GLOWING GLORIES

by

Scott E. Beemer

Black Forest Press
San Diego, California
October, 2002
First Edition

GLOWING GLORIES

by

Scott E. Beemer

PUBLISHED IN THE UNITED STATES OF AMERICA
BY
BLACK FOREST PRESS
P.O. BOX 6342
CHULA VISTA, CA 91909-6342
1-800-451-9404

ACKNOWLEDGEMENT

This book is given by the Holy Spirit in morning
devotions to Scott E. Beemer.

DEDICATION

To "God's Open Forum"
For their inspiration and help.

To the Bride of Christ and to all of the faithful partners working together to spread God's Word and Love.

This book is primarily aimed and dedicated toward teaching,
guiding, and loving the Christians that have not yet risen to the
task the Father has for them.

Disclaimer

This document is an original work of the author. It may include reference to
information commonly known or freely available to the general public. Any
resemblance to other published information is purely coincidental. The author
has in no way attempted to use material not of his own origination. Black Forest
Press disclaims any association with or responsibility for the ideas, opinions or
facts as expressed by the author of this book. No dialogue is totally accurate or
precise.

Printed in the United States of America
Library of Congress
Cataloging-in-Publication

ISBN: 1-58275-114-5

PREFACE

Men are most comfortable doing their own things and taking care of themselves. Too bad it doesn't work all of the time. Our Heavenly Father is much better prepared to give His children just what they need, but do they listen?

The peace and comfort that everyone desires in their heart will only come through dedication and obedience to God's Word. The Holy Spirit brings in this book simple ideas, plans and methods to help each one draw closer to the Father and find the rest that God is holding for his children. Hebrews 4:9

These Holy Spirit notes will help you come to the complete surrender to God without reservation, bringing you into the Love, Joy, and Peace promised. Galatians 5:22

Scott E. Beemer

TABLE OF CONTENTS

SHARE EIGHT: Page 83
Father's Dream, Fate, Kingdom Work, My Way, Believe, A Happy Life, Time, Catching Away, The Ways of Love, Your Way, Word and Way, With Beloved Notes

SHARE NINE: Page 95
Head and Heart, Listening Ear, Free Gift, The End, With Beloved Notes

*Share means what the Holy Spirit is sharing with us.

SHARE ONE

A BALANCING ACT

BELOVED, when you feel low and physically drained turn to Me. Ask for renewal of strength and pay more attention to resting. There is much benefit received when one knows the body's limits. I will never push or drive you in your daily walk. If peace and love seem farther and farther away then bring rest and comfort closer.

All I ever ask is for your attention and love. When I am your focus then the world slips away. Time and energy should go hand in hand. When time seems too short then you usually try to make up for it by using more energy. You are moving out of balance. Learn to pace your time of completion to meet the expiration of your energy. That makes a proper ending and blesses the body with the right time of rest.

If you walk with ME all of the time I will help you with body balance. There is a similar problem of balance with Our time together. You must seek to walk with Me all of the time to stay in the body balance I can give. When I just get part of your time this becomes another way of keeping your soul and body unbalanced with your spirit. Your balancing act causes a lot of physical problems.

When you keep asking Me for a healing and I don't seem to be listening these are some of the problems of interference We experience. Can you now have a better appreciation of how We should be working together? All of the time not just hit or miss as your fancy may lead. Your time assignment is the most important task you have. Not time for breakfast, lunch or dinner but My inclusions into your daily time line.

Make the day start with Us and then just continue. This lesson should assume the importance of "Big Lesson" because around this kind of planning I can build great children with greater promise.

MAKE THIS LESSON A GUIDE TO USING THE
FOLLOWING LESSONS

BELOVED, true growth in the Spirit is only gained through dedication of self, time and flesh. An abundance of understanding only builds towers of sand unless the cement of obedience through action is applied.

BELOVED, dedication is a wonderful practice only when the proper thing is dedicated at the right time. Seek My way early in the morning.

BELOVED, leeway, permission and freedom have I given you, all to test your heart. Searching for truth, struggling for true direction builds My Church on the foundation I desire. A trust established on effort builds a foundation of worth. What kind of a searching soul do you have?

BELOVED, as thoughts of self diminish then Jesus' true love expands. True love is God's love ebbing and flowing creating new thoughts and ways for My children to grow. Everyone is not taught the same way or the same lesson. I do not seek robots; but I seek true love reflected.

BELOVED, much growth occurs when the flesh is abandoned and at rest, then the spirit of man can soar on wings of reflection of Me. This statement is worthy of contemplation.

BELOVED, just a closer walk with Me opens realms of blessings unwrapped. Do not strain or try to imagine, just let your spirit soar. Seek this in the morning.

BELOVED, growth in the Spirit requires a diminishing of self and flesh. All this is a trip of Holy Spirit guidance. Seek this in the morning.

BELOVED, each statement made may not be suitable or timely for everyone. You must desire My guidance to know just what part you should embrace. Seek this in the morning.

BELOVED, it should become obvious to you by now how I intend for you to grow. Seek Me in the morning. Reading the Bible by flesh control should open up your schooling to Holy Spirit leading. If you conquer self and flesh Holy Spirit release is gained.

BELOVED, do you have a growing heart of love? Is there a drawing closer each day in your walk with Me? These are not idle thoughts or suggestions they are vital hints of how to grow.

BELOVED, just when you believe your Christian walk is on track something else seems to distract it. Why is that? My dear ones you will never find the completeness your heart desires until you find all of Me in all of you. Body, soul and spirit must come into perfection. The harmony of Spirit living demands completeness of your flesh, soul and spirit. Have you truly presented your body, soul [mind] and spirit to Me as I asked?

BELOVED, prayers should be love talk between you and Me. Do you have that loving attitude and desire at prayer time? Is your prayer time a much desired and planned for event? Is your prayer time a much longed for and hungered after event?

BELOVED, do you have a great longing in your heart? Is there a desire so strong that it occupies a constant place on your heart? Is your mind drawn to this desire with great frequency? Am I anything like that to you?

BELOVED, do you have a growing heart of love? Is there a drawing closer to Me each day in your walk with Me? These are not idle thoughts or suggestions they are vital hints of how to grow.

BELOVED, never continue to limit Our contact and time together, it is vital for your growth to be more and more open and accepting to My suggestions. Nothing here given is frivolous or worthless; all is vital for your growth. Seek Me in the Bible, seek Me in your heart; Our walk is as close as you will allow.

BELOVED, pay more attention to each other, as you do you will grow closer to Me. Yes seek more of Me through each of MY children. There are blessings given in these manners. You please My heart when you do this.

BELOVED, keep Me on your heart and mind at all times in every circumstance and you will find new avenues of rewards and blessings in places you have never dreamed of or suspected.

BELOVED, the small prices I suggest you pay now are doors of blessings to unfold in your future. Doubt My words and My way and you will find a muddy road filling with rocks and obstacles, you have an enemy lurking.

BELOVED, never give up, never turn away, and as Jesus endured so must every child of God. You must realize the testing daily is a sure sign of your victory to come. Rejoice always singing praises and telling of Jesus' goodness. So shall you be overcomers.

BELOVED, study to be able to view the daily happenings as growth tools given you by a loving Father. All life is short so use what you are given wisely.

BELOVED, every child of God has a prepared path to walk, many of God's children stray from the Father's will, then believe He is causing all of their problems.

BELOVED, many of your blessings daily are hidden in the lives of those around you. As you bring aid, peace and comfort to others you are building rewards and blessings of you own. To keep your eyes centered on others causes God's care to be released about you.

BELOVED, never give thought about how much or how little you may have, realize all you should do is give thanks for your place with the Creator of all things.

BELOVED, it is better to pepper God with praise than to cry out about all your problems. It is better to cry out about all the needs of others than about your own, it is best to give thanks in all things knowing to whom you belong.

BELOVED, there has never been praise and worship to God that has gone unknown or unnoticed by God. In all things give thanks because He always knows, loves and cares about you.

BELOVED, do you think of others' needs first or at all? This may be a good measuring device establishing in your heart just how you are doing with the Father.

BELOVED, you have no concept of the way God the Father watches over you; every thought and desire of your heart is known. You may believe only your actions are measured and counted. You are loved far beyond what you may imagine.

BELOVED, wherever life seems to lead you never stray from

making Me your goal. It's all right to trip and stumble as long as your get up and go is never left behind.

BELOVED, when the carrot you follow is Jesus there will always be a feast to be revealed.

BELOVED, whether your steps are small or they are great strides is of no concern, it's the direction and goal they're taking you to that is all-important.

BELOVED, take these little thoughts as healing pills of love and watch them build you a life healthy, wealthy and wise.

BELOVED, never misjudge the force of small sayings for they carry great potential power if you have the fire to light them off.

BELOVED, keep eager and alert for great gifts of love are bound in small packages.

BELOVED, let the dawn of each day bring a small thread of love to knit us closer. By your attention to what I will bring you, you will find nuggets of silver and gold.

BELOVED, never believe We waste Our time with you each morning, We don't! As you allow, little seeds are planted having marvelous potential.

BELOVED, always build eager anticipation seeking the loving, kind and good to come out of Our time each morning. You will be adding good planks to your ship of life.

BELOVED, never look down when I am your way up; never feel lost when I am always your guide. Never admit failure when I am your goal. Always know to whom you belong.

BELOVED, life and all that it brings you should never be your guide to where I will lead, the way is only your school, make Me your graduation goal.

BELOVED, how shall I let you know how dear you are to Me each day when how near you are is so far away.

BELOVED, try to be one who stands and having done all just stands knowing who I am and who you are to Me.

BELOVED, action is not always growth, and direction is not always sure, keep a tight hold onto My hand.

BELOVED, a quick answer is like a broken pot, it seems to be holding the hot water but?

BELOVED, many times the tried and true will not take you through so don't ignore the new.

BELOVED, what sounds good to your ear may not ring true in your heart, so listen with your spirit too.

BELOVED, do not limit Me to your time, remember who has made time. I use all time and you may too if you will learn to rhyme with My time.

BELOVED, the heart cry of the lost is kept so silent only My Spiritually attuned children are able to answer. You who can hear this silent cry must know that to Me it is a sound so loud.

BELOVED, you must understand to be able to walk the walk I call you to you must hear what the silence has to say.

BELOVED, if you slip, stumble and fall doing My will your bruises will only be badges of honor.

BELOVED, to hear My call your ears maybe plugged up, just keep your heart open.

BELOVED, when I give an order it comes in many wrappings because I desire to please each child with the present of My request.

BELOVED, all I do is aimed to bless and gather My family. What a scattered and hard to hug group they are. What a precious reward are the ones that reciprocate.

BELOVED, what benefit is there to the man that runs ahead of My planning trying to do his own? I allow much leeway in My control over My children, this doesn't mean I allow them complete freedom. Every child of Mine yields to Me out of trusting love, remembers this.

BELOVED, learn to wait upon Me surprising benefits will result. My planning is perfect because I see all, the ahead and the behind. Patience then brings it's own reward. Loving trust is better than gold.

BELOVED, what is better than knowing what will happen in the future? If you knew all wouldn't you feel sure and free? Why then don't you have that kind of trust in your future knowing that I have knowledge of where you are going? Will I not bring you safely through it all?

BELOVED, never tread the path set before you without knowing who's leading you. You will enhance your security by being in constant touch with Me. Rising early, greeting and meeting Me brings your daily directions and satisfies increasing purpose.

BELOVED, when man seeks God it should be with all his might, with all his faith, with all his time, with all of his energy, why isn't this so? Man tries to handle his life day by day by himself, never realizing I could help. My dear children don't be like all the world. Call on Me and I will help.

BELOVED, how do you call on Me? When do you call on Me? Call on Me with all your heart, call on Me all of the time, I am always waiting. Isn't this good news? Why don't you ask and try Me? Give Me all of your time, I give you all of My attention all of the time.

BELOVED, do you ever take one hour and devote it just to Me? Do you ever give Me all of your attention for half of a day? How about taking a whole day and devoting it just to Me? Are these seemingly foolish questions? In reality I am looking for all of your attention all of the time.

BELOVED, when Our time together comes We will be One with each other forever. Do you now understand why We should start Our togetherness now? The sooner We start the better for you.

BELOVED, how many times and how many ways must I use to capture your attention and draw you into your place of forever? Love is My carrot, Love is My way. Patience is My tool, but time is My desire. I will fulfill My desire. I will have My Eternal Family. These notes and messages are all part of My attempt to call you. Will your attention be as perfect as My desire?

BELOVED, never believe that you are ignored or unwanted, it is My life I breathed into you and into everyone else. Will you have consideration for My breath of life? It was given in love and by love it returns, This is a simple picture of gathering Oneness.

BELOVED, learning is a wonderful ability, never misuse or abuse it. Properly handled your learning becomes your vehicle to heaven. Give your learning more time and consideration. As you are obedient to this suggestion I can enhance your learning ability. Test Me and see if this is so!

BELOVED, skills I can give you but motivation you must stir up. Love I can give you but desire to receive opens the door. All growth comes by receiving after desiring. Your trip depends on you, the path I've laid for you, you must find. All victory comes through a determined loving desire. All blessings and rewards I give come from My loving desire.

BELOVED, what a man thinks comes from many sources. His desires are the prime motivator of important decisions. Desires can lead a man to great efforts and accomplishments or to great tragedies. What makes a man? Creator God made man to be an independent thinker giving him self-rule. Death should put man in a position of choice asking what is life and is there something ever-lasting to seek? Just where is your heart's desire taking you?

BELOVED, when a Christian tries to grow in the Lord they face two obstacles. One is time; they must learn to control their time, putting God first in all of their planning. This requires control of self because a good part of the useful time is given to pleasing self. It is obvious then the other problem besides time is the control of self.

BELOVED, the way of winning is begun when the love of the Father is released first in a wave of love for the Father, then for Jesus through time devoted in the word. Control of time will come from love of what you do if what you do is love the Lord. All true growth comes through love, seek love, give love and you'll find love! Love is fast-tracking your way to heaven.

BELOVED, when man desires to grow closer to Me I am always right there waiting. No one surprises Me, I am always aware of what My children are about. If your attention to Me were as con-sistent as My awareness of you We would be One. Love is the well of true desire draw from it.

BELOVED, Do you know how to do the thing I ask? I just gave you a clue "true desire"; you should dwell on that! Then having built a resource of knowledge about true desire, investigate desire until you can detect true love. True love should be the resource of all you do or desire. The love motivator is Me. The love you seek is Me. The love you find, the true love, is Me. BELOVED seek Me, true love, desire Me I am all love; the only true source of love.

BELOVED, seek the Lord of true love, then make true love your Lord. We will have a love walk like none other.

BELOVED, many are the times ahead where you will find upset and confusion, never dwell on these situations, but dwell on Me knowing I have the answers. It's in Our walk of closeness that peace and comfort dwell.

BELOVED, think always about who you are to Me. Think thoughts of praise and victory bringing Me closer all the time. Our Oneness is born in bonding brought by earth's events.

BELOVED, never believe what the eyes may see or what the ears might hear, believe only in what I bring to you. Your growing ability to listen and hear in your Spirit will pave your path to Me with victory.

BELOVED, seldom will earth's peace and comfort bring lasting blessings, only Our growing together daily will prove the way of true love.

BELOVED, the heart of My children will blossom and flower when the Holy Spirit is their source of guidance. The opening of heavenly wonders will bring knowledge flowing from the heart of God.

BELOVED, think with your mind but check with your heart before moving mountains with your speech, have I not said whatsoever you say believing, it will be done for you? Give no thought to the how when it is in obedience to what I say.

BELOVED, your growth in the Spirit is limited only by your belief in the things I say. Study your Bible carefully noting My words of direction for you. Your ability to obey will spring forth as your heart leads your head.

BELOVED, only your growth in your Spirit walk counts in heaven. Visualize your daily walk as a man on a tightrope confidently striding on his small line.

BELOVED, use praise as your daily strength just as you use the air you breath. Spiritual gateways in heavenly places are opened when you do.

BELOVED, try to imagine the love you have inside being bottled up in flesh tortured and tormented. Your love carried in a package rejected and despised because of its appearance. Try to show love out of a container of unworthy appearance. Try to see Jesus through a package of dislike. This was Jesus' neighbor's problem as He grew up to manhood. May His light show through to you.

BELOVED, your knowledge of right and wrong should grow from your close encounter with the source of all truth.

SHARE TWO

I SING

I SING TO THE HEAVENS ABOVE
TELLING FATHER WHO DWELLS THERE,
ABOUT MY UNFOLDING LOVE.

I SING TO THE ONE WHO SAVED ME
TELLING OF HIS WONDERFUL GIFT,
GIVING THANKS FOR MANSIONS I SEE.

I SING AND THE ANGELS REJOICE
TELLING OF JESUS' DEEDS,
AND PRAISING WITH A LOUD VOICE.

I SING AS ANGEL CHOIRS BLEND
TELLING IN SONGS OF WORSHIP,
ABOUT THE LOVE AND JOY I SEND.

I SING WITH LAUGHTER AND PRAISE
TELLING OF ENDLESS TIMES,
KNOWING THAT JOY I RAISE.

BELOVED, how can I reach the real you when you won't keep trying to reach the real Me? How do We level with each other? The partition that needs breaking down is self and free will. I restrain Myself from pushing you and you restrain yourself from giving in completely to Me. Our lives are united at the new birth, the follow on is all left up to your release of self. When you truly seek Jesus and to be like Him then I truly withdraw your obstinate self.

BELOVED, when a man comes to Me I know just how sincere he really is. I never hid from a true seeker. I never stay away from a child who loves Me. My turning away from you is never abandonment. I am quiet when I am watching you. I am silent when I give you opportunity to stretch and grow. I will never hide and stay hidden from My children who love Me.

BELOVED, be very careful about your promises to Me. I carefully watch over and guide all who desire a closer walk. I help and uplift all whose heart desires more of Me.

BELOVED, to a true seeker I open all avenues of growth. I carefully watch and guide a heart that wants more of Me. Sincerity of love is the guide I use to lift up, guard and protect. I will lose none who love Me, no matter how little their knowledge. It all depends on how big their love how far they can go. I will lose none.

BELOVED, when your days are dry and unfruitful don't be upset, worried or concerned. Take each occasion as just another lesson I bring to those I love. Let it test your childlike reaction to the different happenings each day. My peace and calm will prevail through anything coming your way when you are totally mine. Draw strength from all set before you by cloaking yourself in Love and Laughter.

BELOVED, the care I give will always last, that is one reason it seems to come so slowly. When the sure and permanent comes the flighty and temporary leaves. All things are not as they seem, your immediate reaction may not be your best one to believe. My desire is for your permanent well being not your temporary good feeling. You grow as you learn to know Me more.

BELOVED, how can you get to know Me when We never really meet? Obey, just do the things you know you should do; I will trust you with more. Persistence in well-doing builds inner strength that I give. We will never feel close until We have been close with nothing but faith cementing Our relationship. The glue of faith is Our place of birth. Our growth in faith is shown by love released.

BELOVED, how can I make you grow if you do not do the things I say? Partnership is yielding one to another among you and also to Me.

BELOVED, do I not lead and guide those I love, are not the ones who love Me growing and doing My will? Obedience brings rewarding growth.

BELOVED, if you support your Christian brothers will you not support and help those who don't know Me yet? How can you believe you are walking in truth when the truth is your not doing the truth you know?

BELOVED, search your heart, be honest with yourself and admit you know more to do than what you are doing for ME. It is in discipline, self-discipline that I find useful vessels.

BELOVED, wouldn't it be a wonderful busy time if you just pursued and did the things you know you should be doing for Me? Just giving Me the time daily that you haven't enjoyed yet.

BELOVED, this is a lesson in learning from what you observe by understanding things you can't see. Look deep into the heart of a person or a matter with loving interest and searching intent, seeking truth. The things seen or heard may never tell you all truth or any truth.

BELOVED, never rely on your physical senses to tell you truth about Spiritual events or happenings. All truth stems from God; all learning should be sourced from God.

BELOVED, when you seek to learn and grow into a useful tool for Jesus remember to please Him; make Him your only source of learning.

BELOVED, singleness of purpose can generate great power in effort when pleasing Jesus is your reason.

BELOVED, make love the source of all your efforts and you will see your efforts produce great works.

BELOVED, goals are given to make ladders tall and efforts far reaching. Set your goal higher than your own ability, and then call on Jesus' help.

BELOVED, no small effort of loving help is unnoted. The Father watches even your smallest smile or penny given in love.

BELOVED, to always believe you are loved and watched over is faith building on truth.

BELOVED, what a wonder each day can unfold to those of My children who are obedient and open to My calling. Listen My dear ones; listen to My still small voice. I call you to awaken, sleep no more in your dreams but come into My world by your obedience. Learn to live the life inside of you so I can take it outside to the world.

BELOVED, you should stop looking at the things you see and giving them your time. but look at the things unseen as if they were. What I have to reveal is beyond your dreams and into Mine.

BELOVED, please give proper consideration to who you are in Me. For as I am in you, then you will be in me.

BELOVED, never feel that I am leading you where you can't go, I desire to take you where you won't go. Unbelief, distrust, reluctance to believe are all shameful.

BELOVED, forever exists but where it takes you only I know. Shouldn't you have a desire or curiosity to seek? Loving trust is the vehicle of your deliverance, however you must climb aboard on your own to take the ride. Am I not a trustworthy bus driver? Would you rather seek another?

BELOVED, the events unfold carrying the willing ones along in peace and comfort. It is only the hesitant and uncertain that finds trouble and trials of difficulty.

BELOVED, do you truly know how much your future depends on how much you love and trust Me? To the slow, hesitant and uncertain come all the difficulties to support their growing fears.

BELOVED, I have opened the doors of love wide to loving trust, but the doorway becomes narrower and smaller as doubt and unbelief grow. Let your love be so great that all else is overcome. Love is a comforter that no evil can penetrate.

BELOVED, to read these notes is not enough, love of truth must be the oil used to bring knowledge and response into full play.

BELOVED, joy is all your happiness released, and then there is still a lot more joy left over.

BELOVED, if the Spirit realm is real and the angels are real, if they are really real, how real is God to you?

BELOVED, try always try, for by trying you will reveal your strength and weakness, but ask yes ask Me when you try and see the difference. Bring Me into everything you do, yes use the smallest effort and learn to ask My help.

BELOVED, am I not always with you? Come now think and answer truthfully. Yes, I am always with My children all of the time. Just stop and think about that! This is truth, if so why aren't you and I always together in everything you do? I am willing to be a part of all you do, will you let Me?

BELOVED, is My closeness so remote that you don't know it? I have broken down every barrier to be with you right inside, that close. Why aren't you more aware?

BELOVED, in everything acknowledge Me. See My hand with you all of the time. If you never see the result of My presence does that mean I'm not there?

BELOVED, your life now is not to be the completion of My work with you, you are My work in progress. What I will eventually fashion you to be you do not know, just let faith do the "gap filling" for now.

BELOVED, all of Our work together is like a seed planted; not until the final gathering will the farmer know how much he has. Just so with you, leave all with Me after your work in the field is done.

BELOVED, who can tell what kind of a harvest you will gather when you dig into My word putting your heart there?

BELOVED, every seed planted does not grow. Do you know why? Lack of love first. How much love is involved with your seed planting, or do you plant at all?

BELOVED, the use you put these little notes to will determine much in Our relationship. Growth is built with trust, belief, action and work that I am involved in. Only by doing will knowing grow. Only by knowing will love grow, only by love will you grow. Come be a flower in My garden.

BELOVED, does the foolish small thing make any difference to you? Is it overlooked and ignored? What if I put it before you with a great lesson potential? What is the purpose of a note like this? Can it make you more aware of small things that I lay in your path? If you are truly Mine shouldn't you give all occurrences a close look?

SHARE THREE

A WELL OF BLESSINGS

THERE IS A WELL OF BLESSINGS
BURIED DEEP WITHIN,
I GIVE TO ALL MY DEAR ONES
WHO HAVE LEFT THEIR SIN.

I GIVE THIS GIFT AWAITING
EACH MUST FIND THIS WELL,
WHERE I HAVE GIVEN LOVE
FOR ALL TO BREAK THE SPELL.

CAST UPON THE EARTH
THE FLESH IS JUST A PATH,
WHERE I HAVE PUT WELL HIDDEN
A PLACE THAT'S FREE OF WRATH.

THE ONES WHO FIND THE DIPPER
ARE SEEKERS OF ALL TRUTH,
THEY ALL WILL DRINK THIS WATER
AND ALL RECEIVE MY PROOF.

EVERYONE LOOKING FOR LOVE
WILL FIND A PRECIOUS FATHER,
REWARDS AWAITS PERSISTENCE
ALL WHO WILLINGLY DRAW THERE.

A SEEKER

I SEARCH THROUGH PAPERS FOR MONEY,
I LOOK IN MAGAZINES FOR REST.
I RUN AFTER BOOKS TO GUIDE ME,
I KNOW I'M DOING MY BEST.

WHEN I SEE FAILURE DAILY,
I FIND I'M LOSING THIS WALK.
SO WHERE DO I TURN FOR HELP?
WHERE CAN I FIND STRAIGHT TALK?

THE BIBLE IS SAID TO BE HELPFUL,
I'M SURE THEY ALL SEEM SINCERE.
BUT WHEN I READ IT I'M LOST,
WHY DON'T THEY MAKE IT MORE CLEAR?

REST

THERE IS REST FOR THE BODY
A GREAT NECESSITY,
REST ALSO IS SOUL NEEDED
FOR MAKING WHOLE YOU SEE.

BUT LAST OF ALL MOST NEEDED
IS SPIRIT REST WITH GOD,
SO THERE IS REST FOR EVERYONE
UPON THIS OLD EARTH'S SOD.

YOU FIND THIS REST GOD GIVEN
TO MAKE YOUR WAY EACH DAY.
A PEACEFUL PATH LOVE STREWN,
SO ENJOY LIFE WHILE YOU STAY.

BELOVED, every day seems to bring new problems; why don't you look at them as helpful steps in learning? If I am watching over you why don't you just praise and thank Me for all your encounters? I intend to improve you in every manner possible, do you want to grow into Jesus' image? Don't you think I know what I'm doing?

BELOVED, growing is a good thing, you might as well believe that because it will go on for a very long time. I have the time, do you have the patience?

BELOVED, true love never fails; true love always grows. How can that be? Because I am true love.

BELOVED, if these simple lessons are difficult, hard or confusing it is only because of your "self" resisting. Give in to love, love conquers all, I am love.

BELOVED, you see truth through the veil of flesh and twisted by self-pleasing, that is why you can't see Me clearly. I have made a way, seek it!

BELOVED, there is a lot to be said about the benefits of silence. In quiet ideas are born, in silence I can speak, in silence wisdom grows, in stillness love is felt, in peace great gain is experienced. How often are you just in My silence?

BELOVED, great are My hopes and desires for you. Expansive are My plans as you respond in favor. Many are the avenues We can travel. When will you be free to follow Me all of the time?

BELOVED, how high, how far, how long will you stretch at My command? I desire full attention and willing, loving obedience because where I take you, you will be so blessed, and happy and glad you came. It is on wings of trust and belief that you are borne to greater things you have yet to even imagine.

BELOVED, to stay in ignorance is unfruitful. To wallow in self pity is disaster, to enjoy laziness is self-defeating, why don't you try the opposite of all these? Ask Me I can help.

GLORY FOR ALL

I SING IN PRAISE AND WORSHIP,
I SING WITH ALL MY HEART.
I SING IN PRAISE AND WORSHIP,
IT'S THE BEGINNING WHERE I START.

MY PRAISE AND WORSHIP IS ENDLESS,
ABOUT THE ETERNITY WHICH I SING.
MY PRAISE AND WORSHIP ON GOING,
UNTIL ALL THE HEAVENS RING.

AS SONG AND THANKS CONTINUE,
AND ANGEL CHOIRS AGREE.
SONGS AND THANKS KEEP GROWING,
FOR ALL HEAVEN TO WATCH AND SEE.

NOW ALL THE RHYTHM AND RHYME,
BRINGS HEAVENLY HARMONY.
AS RHYTHM AND RHYME RESOUND,
CREATING GLORY FOR ALL TO SEE.

BELOVED, how can I show how much I love you when your love for Me is so slow to grow? This tie between us is on going into forever.

BELOVED, try to draw closer each day. Just take a small step daily because when you look back you will know how far you've come. Hindsight can be a good guide if you will learn from it.

BELOVED, in My hand I hold more than you'll ever need. By holding My hand I can guide you into eternal blessings as yet not listened to or sung.

BELOVED, how fast you grow depends on how well you listen. How well you understand will be revealed in what you do. What you do should show how great I am.

BELOVED, from the fruit of a tree learn a lesson. Out of nothing but a seed in watered dirt comes life. The root gathers strength for sap to rise; the leaves gather power for the fruit to bear. The branches support the bud to blossom and fruit to appear. With fruit showing life in color and taste, no one will know if the fruit goes to waste. How sad this cycle if no one knows. Is this the way your life grows?

TREE FRUIT

A TREE FRUIT TELLS A LESSON,
FROM WATERED SOIL SEEDS GROW.
ROOTS GATHER STRENGTH, SAP RISES,
LEAVES POWER FRUIT TO SHOW.

BRANCHES SUPPORT NEW BUDS,
LIFE SHOWS IN COLOR AND TASTE.
WONDER AND FRAGRANCE ABOUNDS,
HOW SAD THIS CYCLE OF WASTE.

FOR NO ONE KNOWS THIS HARVEST,
AND NO ONE TELLS GOD'S POWER.
THIS TREE JUST STANDS ALONE,
NONE TO SHARE HARVEST'S HOUR.

ARE YOU LIKE A TREE ALONE?
RAISED BY GOD, TO NO ONE SHOWN.
HAVE YOU TOLD OF HIS GREAT POWER,
OR DISPLAYED WHAT YOU HAVE KNOWN?

ARE YOU LIKE FRUIT UNTASTED,
SOFT AND BEAUTFUL WITHIN,
BUT OUTSIDE WORN AND WASTED,
BEATEN BY SATAN AND SIN?

BELOVED, how small is man when you consider his future. The man I bring to Me is far above and beyond the man My children now see. Dear ones have more confidence in Me and you shall surely see the man I wish you to be.

BELOVED, the release of self allows you to soar high above your present dreams, no matter how high you think you can see.

BELOVED, your dreams of My kingdom and place for you should never diminish, just know they will never be as wonderful as the reality I will bring you.

BELOVED, draw closer to Me with every breath and step you can take for this will earn you wonders yet unshown or told. As you believe, learn to receive, and then I can bring you more.

BELOVED, time is like an accordion you can get more out of it if you squeeze and tug and pull. Haven't you packed more pleasure in a few minutes than you could have believed? At other times, haven't the minutes and hours just seemed to drag along? Spend enough time with Me and you will always have more than enough.

BELOVED, what possible good can come from these words written? They are just ink on paper. When put on the printed page, words are just words. What is talk when no one is listening? Both are worthless until an obedient eye or ear is about, and they may be meaningless unless a heart is touched.

BELOVED, can a word, like an arrow, pierce your heart? Like an arrow will it stick or fall off? The word is just a word, but is your heart still the same?

WORDS FLY

WORDS LIKE ARROWS
FLY ACROSS THE SKY,
SOME TO TOUCH HEARTS
OTHERS FALL AND DIE.

SOME WORDS LIKE ARROWS
ARE ALL AFLAME,
THOUGHTS SO WILD
OTHERS BRING SHAME.

WHAT PART DO WORDS
PLAY IN YOUR LIFE,
WILL THEY TURN YOU
TO JOY OR STRIFE?

WILL WORDS GUIDE
AND MAKE YOU STRONG,
OR JUST HURT
AND SHOW YOU WRONG?

CAN WORDS HELP YOU
GROW EACH DAY,
OR NEVER MOVE YOU,
YOU JUST STAY.

BELOVED, to write the words is just a start, to read the words is path walking, but to persist and do the words there is real growth. BELOVED, to love is to extend yourself, stretching out to love will expand the real you, and when love blends with truth and honesty Jesus shows forth.

BELOVED, if to try and fail will make you grow when moved by love, then just think how far trying and succeeding can take you.

BELOVED, no small word of wisdom should ever be lost, who can tell where it came from and why? Write it down, study it, wring out all of its use and watch wisdom grow from just a small seed.

BELOVED, never despise the small and seemingly insignificant. It may be just a word, a look, sometimes a feeling; I may be speaking to your heart.

BELOVED, sometimes to be slow and thoughtful is really being God like, or God led. It takes time for a picture to become clear. The fog of reality must burn away as the sunshine of love increases.

BELOVED, to move hastily is to strew a path with rocks while a slow response allows love and understanding to grow. Many problems have a field of obstacles, some hidden, some unclear, some camouflaged and some so complex as to defy understanding. Call on Me, wait in prayer, and seek My report. Nothing laid at My feet will bring you defeat.

BELOVED, when will We become a team? Just you and Me together in everything you do every day? Make this a goal, plant this desire in your heart, and keep it in focus always.

BELOVED, remember where I am love is, where love is no evil will prevail!

WHERE FROM, WISDOM?

WHERE DOES WISDOM COME FROM?
IS THERE A SOURCE OF SUCH WORTH?
HOW WILL MAN EVER FIND
THIS PLACE OF WISDOM'S BIRTH?

CAN HE SEARCH OUT THE HEAVENS?
CAN MAN SCOUR ALL OF THE EARTH?
HOW IN THE WORLD WILL MAN
EVER MAKE COMPLETE THIS SEARCH?

WITHOUT A GOD IN HEAVEN,
WITHOUT A GOD ON LAND,
HOW WILL MAN BE ABLE
TO FIND WHERE WISDOM STANDS?

BELOVED, you should never come before Me doubting or wondering if I can hear you. Faith is the line of Our connection. I never lose My line to you, but do you let your line go dead?

BELOVED, I desire for you to keep Me close in everything you do, I'm always there anyway. I just don't reveal Myself when you don't acknowledge Me, or when I'm watching you to see how true you really are to Me. My children know I'll never leave or forsake them, never!

BELOVED, love is a many faceted wonder, My love goes far beyond man's knowledge, dreams, thinking, or imagination. Just as man will never fully know all of Me, My love is greater still.

BELOVED, work, strain, desire, and never stop trying to know, capture, hold, and keep My love. I give and give forevermore all My love you can desire, hold, or ever need, and still there's more.

BELOVED, how long can a man go without knowing Me? Just as long as he wants. I put no demand on man to seek Me, but it is My heart's desire that he will. I put no restrictions on man about telling others about Me; they can talk about Me all they want. If you are My child then you should have a desire to tell of My love. Do you have a desire, do you tell?

BELOVED, no man is ever all alone, unless he wills and desires to be. My heart cries out to the lonely and lost does yours? You may gage your love for Me by your love for others. Do you pray for salvation for the lost? Do you seek out the lost to win them for Me? My children know My love and want to spread it to the lost and lonely. This is My most urgent desire at this last time for the gathering.

OH JESUS

OH JESUS, JESUS, JESUS
THE ONLY HELP WE NEED.
HE STAYS RIGHT HERE WITH US,
THROUGH HIM WE WILL SUCCEED.

OH JESUS, JESUS, JESUS
OUR CRIES OF HELP RINGS OUT.
YES LORD YOU KNOW OUR NEED,
YOU KNOW WHAT WE'RE ABOUT.

OH JESUS, JESUS, JESUS
WHEN THAT DAY APPEARS.
WHEN HEAVEN BURSTS UPON US,
AND ALL EVIL DISAPPEARS.

OH JESUS, JESUS, JESUS
ETERNITY JUST AHEAD.
EVERYTHING RINGS TRUE,
EVERYTHING YOU SAID.

COME JESUS, JESUS, JESUS
BRING YOUR WILL TO PASS.
GIVE US YOUR SALVATION,
ETERNITY AT LAST.

BELOVED, never doubt and you'll always have the love I give. My love smoothes the way, My love will make each day.

NEVER DOUBT

BELOVED NEVER DOUBT
THE LOVE THAT I GIVE
AND YOU'LL NEVER BE WITHOUT.
WILL BE THE WAY TO LIVE.

BELOVED ALWAYS BELIEVE
AND KEEP ME VERY NEAR.
MY CLOSE PRESENCE
CHASES AWAY ALL FEAR.

BELOVED ALL YOUR GROWTH
IS SAFELY IN MY HANDS.
ALWAYS IN MY ARMS
YOU SHOULD TAKE YOUR STAND.

BELOVED YOU ARE SURROUNDED
WITH ALL MY LOVING CARE.
JUST KNOW, ALWAYS BELIEVING
I KEEP YOU SAFELY THERE.

BELOVED, how easily you drift away and forget all these things I bring you. Never let the world be that intrusive.

SHARE FOUR

DRIFTING

DEARLY BELOVED NEVER
DRIFT FROM WHERE YOU ARE,
FOR IT MAKES THE RETURNING
MUCH HARDER BY FAR.

CAN'T YOU TELL YOU'RE SLIPPING
WHEN DISTANCE SETTLES IN?
DON'T YOU KNOW YOU'RE
RETURNING BACK TO SIN?

MY CHILD I PUT WITHIN YOU
SAFE GUARDS THAT ARE SO SURE,
WHY DO YOU ABOUND IN WAYS
RETURNING TO WHERE YOU WERE?

HOLDING TIGHT WHILE MOVING
TAKE MY HAND EACH DAY,
ALL ALONG MY PATHWAY
ARE SAFE PLACES TO STAY.

KNOWING IN YOUR HEART
IS WHERE I PUT MY TRUST,
KEEPING ME SO CLOSE
YOU'LL FIND BECOMES A MUST!

BELOVED, how many times have you lost peace that I have given you? Yes, I give you peace My dear ones when you need rest, but do you know and receive it? My peace is always ready just as My love is always there for you but do you believe, wait on Me or desire My help? Seek My presence more, seek My still small voice, seek to draw closer to Me, I am always waiting.

BELOVED, do you truly accept Me, just sometimes, maybe? Just when trouble comes? Just when you have time? How much am I desired?

BELOVED, these little notes are last time notes of love calling all who will read them to choose now where they want to spend eternity.

HEART'S CRY

OH HOW OFTEN JESUS CRIES
WHEN HE SEES THE CHILDREN LOST.
HOW OFTEN DOES HE SEEK
REPAYMENT FOR WHAT IT COST?

TO SAVE ALL OF MANKIND
HAS NOT WORKED OUT COMPLETE,
BECAUSE IT SEEMS TO GOD
MAN JUST DESIRES DEFEAT.

DO YOU HEAR AND ANSWER
THE CRY FROM JESUS' HEART?
DOES YOUR RESPONSE IN LOVE
MAKE HIM REGRET THE START?

TO BRING ALL MEN TO GOD
HAS ALWAYS BEEN THE PLAN,
BUT THE FATHER HAS A CHORE
BELIEVING THAT HE CAN.

FOR MAN IS SO REBELLIOUS
GOD HAS SOME REGRET STORED UP,
WILL JESUS AND THE FATHER
SET WITH MEN AND SUP?

COME NOW ALL YOU WHO HEAR
MAKE YOUR CHOICE REAL SOON,
FOR SHORTLY COMES THE TIME
WHEN YOU MAY JUST CHOOSE DOOM?

BELOVED, never think you have all the time in the world to decide who you will believe, or where you choose to go, the Father has a schedule firm and without change set before the world. Right now you should be aware of His door closing on this age.

BELOVED, many a man is saved by following his heart and leaving his head behind.

THE GIFT GIVEN

GOD HAS GIVEN THE GIFT,
THE LIFE OF HIS ONLY SON,
TO SAVE ALL MEN FOREVER,
EVEN WERE THERE ONE.

YES, JESUS' GIFT WAS GIVEN,
SO EVERY MAN COULD KNOW,
THAT GOD HAS CREATED,
LIFE FOR MAN TO SHOW.

THE LOVE THE FATHER HAS,
THE GIFT THAT KEEPS ON GIVING,
SO EVERY CHILD OF GOD,
WOULD HAVE A LIFE WORTH LIVING.

NOW MAN'S PART IS TO CHOOSE,
JUST WHAT HE WANTS TO BE,
TO FAIL ALL BY HIMSELF,
OR ACCEPT GOD'S VICTORY.

BELOVED, the simple call upon these pages has eternal time plans displayed showing God's call to His children. Are you hearing and moving as you should? Never misjudge the simple effort here shown.

BELOVED, when will joy be ever present, when will love be never lacking, when will peace be all around, when will We be together in truth? Soon dear ones soon, for before the pleasure must come task completion. The Father calls each one to obedient love displayed. Seek your place of performance, practice and learn it well to be worthy of God's rewards for you.

BELOVED, never doubt your place with the Father, doubt dissolves faith and will bring to an end perfect results. Know the Father as the source of all perfection.

BELOVED, small tasks can bring out great talent when done in love. Test this in all you do. Your growth is in your hands, be sure in whose hands you are.

BELOVED, to doubt is a step in error, to correct an error is to learn and grow. To live without doubt is to follow truth without fault.

MISSIVE LOVE

SHOULD I WRITE TO YOU EACH DAY,
WOULD THERE BE ENOUGH TO SAY?
WOULD I FIND A NEW JOY SPRINGING,
COULD I FIND RELEASE IN SINGING?

CAN I WRITE TO YOU NEW THINGS,
TELL OF BIRDS WITH COLORFUL WINGS.
OPEN CLOUDS WITH COLORS BURST,
BRING BEAUTY, SATISFYING THIRST?

OPEN HEAVEN FOR ME TO SEE,
AND TELL HOW DEAR YOU ARE TO ME.
ALL MY HEART'S DESIRE DISPLAYED,
PRESENTS PILED, AT YOUR FEET LAID.

COULD A HEART-FELT LETTER SENT,
EVER SHOW THE PURE INTENT?
CAN PEN DISPLAY TRUE HEART'S DESIRE,
MAKE PLAIN ALL YOU INSPIRE?

COULD JUST A LETTER EVER BE,
A BLESSED JOY FOR YOU TO SEE?
CAN INK AND PAPER CARRY LOVE,
CAN DREAMING PEN BE SEEN ABOVE?

BELOVED, when I talk there should be listening ears, do you listen? I have many sage and wonderful words to give to My people, but they will not listen. My dear ones, will you listen? How can We grow closer without the speaking voice and the listening ear?

BELOVED, time is running out, the lessons to save must be short. How can they know if they aren't told, how can they be told if they won't listen? Time I give but time must end to bring the new beginning. Pray for listening ears.

BELOVED, how I long for every one to come into the world of wonders that I have in restraint been holding back. I am anxious for release; "obedience" needs release and freedom to act. Seek to draw closer to Me each moment I give you. Can't you feel the need; don't you know the times?

ANTICIPATION

WITH GREAT ANTICIPATION
YES, WITH HOPE AND JOY,
I SPREAD OUT WITH INTEREST
KNOWLEDGE I DEPLOY.

TO WIN AND SAVE SO MANY
THAT MEN CAN NEVER COUNT,
FOR OVER THE WHOLE EARTH
ONLY I WILL KNOW THE AMOUNT.

SOULS TO WIN AND HARVEST
PRECIOUS, LARGE AND SMALL,
YES, EVERYONE WILL HEAR
THE MESSAGE IS FOR ALL.

COME UNTO JESUS NOW
THERE ISN'T MUCH TIME LEFT,
YOU KNOW ALL THE TRUTH
SALVATION IS MY GIFT.

TELL ALL WHO WILL LISTEN
THAT AN END IS COMING SOON,
TO MISS THIS SALVATION
CAN ONLY END IN DOOM.

BELOVED, the time is coming and is almost here when suddenly you will know, but will you have time and ability to receive?

Now you still can make it, now you still can grow. Come into My arms quickly and reap what I have sown. Eat of the good things of the harvest do not wait for only scraps that are hard to find. How much plainer can I get? You say what are you talking about? Read what has been given these last days.

BELOVED, let love be ever present in your life. Make love and laughter a way for all you do. Love smoothes the road, love removes rocks and obstacles in your path, love protects.

BELOVED, the love walk is rare few can find and walk the walk of true love. True love has power; true love is given from the Father to fill the heart to receive all the Father desires for that special vessel. Seek true love, be a true love seeker. The Father searches hearts across the world looking for that true love seeker.

MAKE DAY DREAMS REAL

DOES NIGHT HOLD MAGIC FOR YOU,
IS SLEEP A WALK THROUGH DREAMS?
DO YOU SEE THINGS FROM HEAVEN,
ARE DREAMS REAL LIVING SCENES?

CAN YOU CONTROL WHAT HAPPENS,
OR ARE YOU A PERSON LED?
IS THERE SOME POWER WORKING,
DO YOU HEAR ALL THAT'S SAID?

WHY THEN DO DREAMS OCCUR,
ARE YOU THE ONLY ONE?
HAVE NIGHT DREAMS ANY PURPOSE,
DO THEY TEACH OR ARE THEY FUN?

IF NIGHT DREAMS GIVE YOU PLEASURE,
CAN YOU CONTROL WHAT'S DONE?
MAYBE THEY END SUDDENLY,
YOU NEVER KNOW WHO WON.

I'M SUGGESTING A NEW PATH,
TRY LIVING DREAMS EACH DAY.
CALL ON ME TO LEAD AND GUIDE,
MAKE YOUR DAY A LOVING WAY.

THE LOVE I BRING IS NEW,
YOU HAVE A JOY TO FEEL.
SHOWING LOVE TO ALL,
YOU MAKE MY LOVE SO REAL.

KEEP ME ALWAYS ON YOUR MIND,
RECEIVE THE DREAMS I GIVE,
KNOWING GROWING IN THIS WAY,
YOU'LL FIND TRUE LIFE TO LIVE.

BELOVED, never be fully satisfied with what you can do and always be satisfied with what the Father does through you. Yes know the difference; it is not your love that counts it is God's love flowing through you that is true love working. Seek, seek ever be seeking for that love release from the Father. This is the search the Father rewards.

BELOVED, not by your strength, not by your power but by My love saith the Lord. Let all things come to you and through you in the strength and power of My love. A love vessel at work is most blessed and is a blessing to all.

BELOVED, be blind to earth's ways and patterns, concentrate on only what I bring you. You must learn to know the difference. I work from inside out; the world will work from the outside in. What are you doing inside?

BELOVED, now is the time to be used, as never before, now is My call released that all may hear, and now is the testing of who hears and then does.

BELOVED, to be blessed with a listening ear comes to many but to do is dependent on only the obedient love in each heart. My love and help is spread abroad freely, it is the reaction in each heart that determines the tasks and goals. I will lead, encourage, guide and help everyone but everyone responds differently. This difference is part of God's plan, how far it takes each person is left to each one's drive and efforts. Yes there are very special people; you should seek out why they are special and learn and grow by what you find.

BELOVED, these little notes can lift you high or expose your lack of worth. Please use them properly and I will help all honest efforts given. Seek to make a wonder trip of every suggestion given. Let Me be revealed more clearly in each "BELOVED".

BELOVED, I give My time and attention to each note hoping to turn many hearts toward a better life with Me. I am blessed when you read, understand and grow. Many of My lost children will be saved by the listening, reacting, and doing ones, make My day by obeying this word given and I will make each of your days worth living. Test Me and try Me, you will grow the more you obey what I am teaching.

SHARE FIVE

LIVING THE DAY

SOME PEOPLE JUST EXIST,
MOVING BY REACTION,
NEVER THINKING LOVE,
BECOMING A NEGATIVE FACTION.

WHERE IS YOUR TRAIL GOING?
DO YOU KNOW OR HAVE A PLAN?
WHAT REALLY LEADS AND GUIDES YOU,
OR IS YOUR LIFE A SHAM?

JESUS CAME WITH LOVE,
DIRECT FROM THE FATHER.
I'M SHOWING YOU THE WAY,
IF YOU'LL ONLY BOTHER.

KEEP THE BIBLE OPEN,
READ AND BELIEVE EACH PAGE.
THEN I'LL BE RIGHT BESIDE YOU,
OPENING YOUR CAGE.

YES, SETTING FREE YOUR SPIRIT,
THROUGH NEW BIRTH YOU LIVE.
RELEASE ALL SELF TO GROW,
AND REJOICE BY WHAT YOU GIVE.

LOSE YOUR SELF IN JESUS,
NEW LOVE WILL HELP YOU GROW,
AS JOY AND LOVE INCREASES,
BY DOING ALL I SHOW.

OBEDIENCE BECOMES A BLESSING,
AND YOUR LIFE REVEALS THE TRUTH,
AS JESUS LEADS AND GUIDES,
MAKING YOU A LIVING PROOF.

BELOVED, never dismiss the suggestions I give you, behind all of My ways is the power of My desire, let that become the driving force motivating all that you do. Think about this, there is great power and help behind obedience with rewards untold.

BELOVED, come and let's reason together, all of My ways are very reasonable. You must learn about reasoning. Think now what does reasoning mean? True reasoning will only come from Me. You must spend reasonable time with Me. I must be the reason for the things that you do. The things you do must be because I gave you a reason to do them. Make Me the reason behind, and motive for every thing you purpose. It takes thought and loving care to determine to do the reasonable way of accomplishing a task. Does all of this sound reasonable?

BELOVED, the time spent reading these notes should become days of concentrated effort obeying them.

BELOVED, to dismiss the wisdom here flowing is like cutting off your feet and trying to run. Never overlook these blessings in disguise, but search your heart for obedience and you'll find My help unending.

BELOVED, once you find the true source of everything shouldn't you strive to know all about this place of your birth, shouldn't you be seeking all knowledge knowing it's worth? This is the ultimate question before man. The right answer settles his way forever. Jesus is the right answer, are you a right answer seeker?

ALWAYS KNOW

MANY WAYS LIE BEFORE MAN
HE PICKS AND CHOOSES
WHAT HE CAN.

NEVER BELIEVE HE LIVES ALONE
SEARCH THE THINGS
THAT HE HAS SOWN.

LOOK BENEATH THE SURFACE
OBVIOUS PLANS MAY
DISGUISE HIS PURPOSE.

I HIDE MY DESIRES
IN MANY WAYS
WATCHING WHAT TRANSPIRES.

DON'T BELIEVE MAN IS ALONE
YOU CAN KNOW
BY WHAT HE'S SOWN.

IS IT WRATH AMD HATE
BRINGING TO MAN
HIS SURE FATE?

OR IS THERE LOVE
A SPECIAL TRAIT
COMING FROM ABOVE?

YOU SHOULD ALWAYS KNOW
THE TRUE LOVE SOURCE
OF WHAT YOU SOW.

IT BEHOOVES EVERYONE
TO SEEK THE SOURCE
FROM THE SON.

BELOVED, why strain and try on your own strength to do what's right in your sight? Keep everything in My sight and I will cause you to do what's right.   View from MY perspective and cover the scene with love.

BELOVED, when your trying becomes a strain let go and let God. Yes try putting more of your situations in My hands. How, you ask? Simply by learning to be led by your Holy Spirit. Look on each challenge through the eyes of My love. Try solving problems with My love answer. Call on Me and I will answer readily, try Me and see.

BELOVED, when you read these notes is it with the hunger of desire to learn? Why are you bothering? Do you sincerely want to draw close? Then practice what I tell you and I will know your heart and help all your endeavors.

BELOVED, it is with joy and pleasure that I would train you, why must you wait until great difficulties arise before you call? Our walk in pleasant times can build a rapport supporting you in the unpleasant occasions.

BELOVED, how can I serve you best? What is your need now that you will share with Me? Isn't that what friends are for?

WHAT A FRIEND

DO YOU EVER HAVE A PICTURE
IN YOUR HEART OF A NEED?
DO YOU SEE YOU LOSING,
OR WILL YOU SUCCEED?

HAVE YOU HELP AWAITING
IN A FRIEND SO CLOSE?
JUST CALL AND YOU KNOW,
HE'LL HELP YOU THE MOST.

A FRIEND THAT TRULY CARES
ALWAYS SHOWING LOVE.
A FRIEND THAT'S ALWAYS THERE,
CLOSER THAN A GLOVE.

A FRIEND THAT KNOWS YOUR HEART
ONE WATCHING EVERY TIME,
NEVER MISSES CARING,
WITH YOU IN PERFECT RHYME.

JESUS FILLS THIS PICTURE
A FRIEND SO VERY CLOSE.
ONE IF HE WAS ABSENT,
YOU'D MISS HIM THE MOST.

BELOVED, keep Me closer than your closest lover; keep Me
closer than your very breath. Always keep Me with you in your
heart and in your mind. That way you will be practicing the eternal
life We'll live. Yes, dear ones, there are many important things you
should be doing with the short time you have left, but this word is
giving you the most important test.

BELOVED, the final and last gathering of God's Golden Garden of Heaven's Harvest is now beginning. Each child of Jesus will have revelation of this time. The call is universal and without reservations. NOW God's heart is open as never before and the arms of heaven it's self are prepared for the children's "Spurt Growth" into Jesus.

The call from Jesus will echo within each willing one. Call out to Jesus in complete surrender now and the Bride's Garmenting will begin. The undergarments require all loss of self and complete surrender to Jesus. As you ask for this in all sincerity and make Jesus the desire of your heart the Father is able to impart the gift requested. This first step is the way of final surrender. The imparting of the mind of Jesus and the receiving of His likeness is basic to any further growth.

Every child of God will follow this path as outlined. The gift of Jesus is the Garmenting of the Bride. This is the perfecting of the Bride. This is the fulfilling of the Bible scriptures "You shall be Holy for I am Holy"; " You shall be perfect as I am perfect"; " You shall see Me and know Me for you will be like Me".

LOVE TIME GATHERING

MAY EVERY LIVING CHILD OF GOD
BRING THEIR HEART TO JESUS,
OPENLY MAKING DECLARATION,
KNOWING GOD BELIEVES US.

END TIMES COME ONLY ONCE
AND THEN RESULTS APPEAR,
EXPOSING TRUTH AND WINNING
HEARTS AWAY FROM FEAR.

GOD'S WORK IS NEVER OVER
AND SOON THIS TRUTH WILL SHOW,
WHEN SOULS ARE LEFT AWAITING
WHILE WILLING ONES ALL GO.

INTO THE HEART AND LIFE
PLANNED FROM GOD'S BEGINNING,
FOR EVERYONE THAT'S WILLING
WILL HAVE A HAPPY ENDING.

BELOVED, your complete surrender is God ordained, God planned, God desired, God inspired, you must call out now for all of Jesus. Let yourself be made into what you know in your heart you were fashioned to be. Say "Jesus take all of Me, I give myself up completely without reservation to You". Come into My heart as never before. Do this new thing right now in Me. Father I thank you for this restoration without reservation.

BELOVED, never doubt when God calls you out, His planning is always perfect, just remember that's you " Just like Jesus".

BELOVED, the things of heaven will not be too strange because I've shown My pattern here on earth. The earth and heaven are all mine I've made heaven just a little finer for now. My dear ones draw closer to Me here on earth it will make your entry into heaven so much sweeter and neater.

BELOVED, the time you devote to Me now, learning about Me ,will pay much greater dividends than if you wait and learn in heaven. Now your attention means much more to Me and allows Me greater latitude in blessing you. Some growth is limited later on. Your "earth learned" blessings have great impact on your heavenly place

BELOVED, wax filled ears are just the same to you as not listening. Ears that hear are just as useless to you as not obeying what you hear or read. Pray and ask for My help. Seek My help in listening and obeying; I will always assist a willing child of Mine.

BELOVED, how the heart of God cries out to all of His children from all He has made. His heavens show His handiwork and the earth His loving care. My dear ones wake up your whole being to know who you are to Him, [Creator of everything.] You are His desire, His children, and His eternal loving family. After He has brought you who respond into the total awareness of His being, He then releases you to be like Him. He opens His universe and gives it to you, heirs and joint-heirs with Jesus. No writer writes, no painter paints, no capability of man can ever explore or expose the wonders to be man's when obedience and love brings the eyes of man to see what "Abba Father's" heart has planned and produced.

BELOVED, when you give Jesus time now there has never been written the blessings and rewards to be given at your total surrender. What you miss by not obeying will never be shown to you, wouldn't you prefer receiving this unknown rather than finding out and knowing eternal damnation?

BELOVED, how can you continue to resist all that is shown to you in the Bible? Surrender brings sure blessings by faith, healing, patience, love, joy, happiness, eternal life all are laid at your feet. Where will your hard heart take you?

THE HARD HEART

THERE IS A PART OF MAN
THAT SEEMS SO STRONG AND SURE,
A STRENGTH IN SELF'S HEART
WHICH BATTLES NEVER CURE.

HOW POSITIVE AND WELL YOU ARE
HOW CLEVER AND HOW SMART,
YES, THERE'S NOTHING YOU CAN'T DO
YOU FINISH EVERYTHING YOU START.

THIS WORLD IS YOURS TO CONQUER
YOU HAVE ALL YOU NEED TO WIN,
IN YOURSELF YOU'RE HAPPY
AND YOU'RE OVERCOMING SIN.

BUT WHERE'S THE STRENGTH
OF YOUR YOUTHFUL PAST,
WHY CAN'T YOU SEE AND DO?
WHY DON'T YOUR THINGS LAST?

WHAT'S GOING ON AS YOU FADE
TRYING AS YOU WOULD?
EVERYTHING GETS HARDER
YOU CAN'T DO AS YOU SHOULD.

OLD AGE SEEMS MUCH HARDER
THAN YOU EVER THOUGHT,
YOU WONDER WHAT'S WITH LIFE
WHAT HAVE YOUR STRUGGLES BOUGHT?

BELOVED, only your good decisions now will pave your path with pleasure. To receive Jesus is your entry into wonders never known or conceived. Only Bible study with the Holy Spirit teaching will guide you into your wonder way with Jesus. Test Jesus' plan and never consider again the ways of man.

YOUR GUIDE

THERE IS A PLAN WELL HIDDEN
THAT MEN MUST SEEK TO KNOW,
IT LIES WITHIN HIS REACH
BUT ONLY GOD CAN SHOW.

YOU MUST HAVE A GREAT DESIRE
NOT JUST A PASSING FANCY,
TO SEEK THE PEARL OF WISDOM
AND GO WHERE MAN CAN'T SEE.

THERE'S HIDDEN IN MAN'S HEART
A SPECIAL PLACE OF WISDOM,
ONLY FOUND BY SEARCHING
IN GOD'S HOLY KINGDOM.

HOW TO BREAK THE BARRIER
OF MAN'S RELUCTANT SOUL,
WILL TAKE A MIGHTY ACT
OF MAKING GOD YOUR GOAL.

SO ASK THE LORD JESUS
TO COME INTO YOUR HEART,
THAT WILL PUT ALL HEAVEN
CHEERING AT YOUR START.

BELOVED, why cry and feel sorry for yourself when things don't go your way, maybe just maybe, there is a lesson in this showing you more of My hand upon you. Look for the good under, behind, on top of and some place around the problem. Praising and giving thanks in all things, remember when you react in the manner I have taught you there is the greatest victory you can have.

BELOVED, each little lesson can be the cord binding Us closer each day. Never doubt that you are mine and I am yours. It is your confirming Our relationship each day that stabilizes and keeps Us close.

BELOVED, always keep the Bible close to your hand and heart, remember I will always speak to you in some way by word, by voice, by reading, by people, by situations, or by your heart within you. Learn to be obedient to all these possibilities. We will have a great time growing in Oneness.

BELOVED, try with all of your faculties and watch your growth blossom. Love ever fails.

LOVE MY LOVE

HOW CAN A PERSON KNOW
JUST WHERE AND WHEN HE'LL GO?

INTO THE UNKNOWN DEATH
WHEN HE'LL LOSE ALL BREATH?

LIFE CAN BE SO SHORT
JUST WHEN WILL HE ABORT?

WOULDN'T IT BE VERY KIND
IF LOVE WAS ALL YOU WOULD FIND?

WHERE IS YOUR TRUST IN WHAT I SAY
DON'T YOU KNOW LOVE IS THE WAY?

GIVE TO ME EACH PRECIOUS MOMENT
WRAPPED IN LOVE JUST SO YOU'LL KNOW IT.

LET LOVE, MY LOVE BE ALL YOU KNOW
AND YOU WILL SEE WITH LOVE YOU'LL GO!

BELOVED, when all lessons are done and you come into your final rest you must know My love is best. Taste and see how good it'll be.

BELOVED, start each day with praise and thanksgiving, this will help set things right and I will carefully guide you. Always trust My presence and love whether you "feel" it or not. Always go by My word to find My love. It is your faith causing My release of love. My love is always available but your wall is sometimes up.

BELOVED, My rest, My peace, My love where are they in your daily walk? They are always ready, available and waiting. It is your right to receive or reject all that I have for you; yes, you can stop the flow of all My blessings by your desire. Watch the words of your mouth, haven't I said speak to the mountain and believe and you shall have what you say? You must pay more attention to what I say and to what you say. We have great power.

BELOVED, as truth is revealed power is given, as power is given responsibility is demanded, never feel so free that you think I don't know everything you think and do.

BELOVED, try, try and try again until you hear My voice, listen deep inside where a calm and peace lie, seek to find in there a way. I have for you a special task. A place that only you can fill don't you know you are special to Me? Yes, this is to My children all who read and believe; you are MY special ones, you who are obedient.

BELOVED, your life is to be directed by Me, but in love not yet revealed. When your desire for Me reaches the place you hear and obey then We will seek to draw you into the walk of love. How can this be told when you will not listen; how can your life come into order when you are not obeying Me? You are not bad, you are not disobedient but you have not given Me the release I need. Ask and it will be given, seek and it will be found, knock and the door to wonders will open, but make Me your single desire!

WHO? WHAT?

WHAT IS DESIRE BUT A CARROT DANGLED?
WHAT IS A WANTING BUT PASSING FARE?
WHAT IS SEEKING WITHOUT PURPOSE?
WHY AM I GOING THERE?

ALL LOOKS VAIN WITH USELESS EFFORT.
I SENSE A GROWING LOSS.
ALL THINGS SEEM SO GOOD THEN CHANGE.
LIFE APPEARS JUST A COIN TOSS.

WHO MADE ME AND THIS PLACE?
WHO IS GUIDING THIS FOOLISH WAY?
WHO IS WATCHING AND WHO CARES?
WHO AM I AT THE END OF DAYS?

JUST WHAT LIES SO FAR AHEAD?
JUST WHERE IS MY LIFE GOING?
JUST WHEN WILL PROMISE SHOW?
JUST WHAT HAVE I BEEN SOWING?

OH GOD, IF YOU ARE SOME PLACE REAL,
OH GOD, WHERE DO YOU HIDE?
OH GOD, SOME SAY YOU LIVE
BUT WHERE COULD YOU ABIDE?

I CRY OUT IN WONDER SHOWING.
I CRY OUT IN IGNORANCE MORE.
I CRY OUT TO WHO OR WHAT?
ALL I SEE IS AN EMPTY SHORE.

WHERE CAN LIFE BE TAKING ME?
WHERE MUST ALL THIS GO?
WHERE IS THERE AN ANSWER SURE?

WHEN IS THERE A TIME I KNOW?

BELOVED, do you have any love for those that are lost? Do you ever really ask Me to give them help? Do you consider how alone and frightened many are? Do you ever really care? You can make a place for yourself by just praying for the lost. Where could your love for the lost take you? Have you ever thought about that?

BELOVED, try to always be aware of how close I am to you and how much I care about everything you do. This is truth many find hard to accept. It is your believing binding Our Oneness by faith. Love is then confirmed.

BELOVED, each little note is intended to show Our love for you and to give you help most needed. Remember you will not grow by just doing your own thing. All true growth comes from complete release of self and complete acceptance of My guidance. All My ways for you are in your hands, by faith you hear Me, by faith you believe, by faith you obey.

BELOVED, learn to walk the love walk. My love bottled up in you is worthless, your love by it's self is useless, only when you allow My love to freely flow through you will We be doing Our thing.

BELOVED, always see Us as a team; We should always be One in every effort. You will learn your way by doing My way. Your training is purposeful, meaningful and most useful. Your obedience brings great blessings to others and is building rewards in your future.

BELOVED, see your growth as Our growth. The Father has set a place and a plan just for you. It is My task to lead, guide, aid and help you in any way I can; it is your hesitation and lack of willingness holding Us back.

SHARE SIX

THE FATHER'S PLACE AND PLAN

EVERY PARENT HAS A HEART
YEARNING TO HELP THEIR CHILDREN.
GOD IS THE SAME, FILLED WITH CARE
ALWAYS TRYING TO LEAD SOME.

JUST AS YOU ALREADY KNOW
THE OFFSPRING SEEMS SO FAR AWAY,
THAT EVEN GOD WILL GIVE UP
TO COME BACK ANOTHER DAY.

HE HAS HIS PLAN AND PLACE TO GO
FOR EVERY CHILD HE LOVES,
BUT MAKING THEM SIT STILL AND LEARN
TAKES GOD AND ALL HIS ANGELS ABOVE.

THE GATHERING AT HOME AT LAST
IS ALWAYS ON GOD'S HEART,
BUT WHY MUST ALL OF HIS WORK
SEEM LIKE IT'S LATE TO START?

GOD WILL NEVER QUIT OR TIRE
HE'LL BE THERE AT THE END,
LOVING, CARING, GATHERING ALL
INTO HIM WE ALL WILL BLEND.

BELOVED, how can words express heart felt Spiritual desires? The language of men is so limited in revealing things of the Spirit. To make word pictures of God's heart's desires is like making a painting and having only black paint available!

BELOVED, just because the mind of man is earthly limited does not mean God can't communicate with him. It is the free wheeling free will keeping man apart more than a limited mind. You see there is the heart of man to capture requiring God's attention. Do you have a mind for God? Have you checked where your heart is?

BELOVED, the heart reveals it's self by the life man leads. Man's mind is following man's heart when pleasing flesh is apparent. When man loves "things" more than God that is a revelation of man's heart. Can you control your flesh to obey the Bible? Where is your time spent and on what?

BELOVED, by the works of man, man reveals to God just where he is concerning his Spiritual growth. Wealth building is a fine endeavor when God's purposes are the goal. When riches and more riches becomes the only way of a man he is fast separating himself from God.

BELOVED, have you really tried to analyze your true desires? Most men can't recognize a true desire. It is a one purpose, one goal, and one direction drive taking all effort, wealth, time and attention. There are very few who strive in such a manner. However as an illustration that points out an all consuming "true desire"; if a man would make a like effort seeking the Father can you even imagine the results? What if I said to you follow that way seek God? Now stop and consider that approach. Is there really anything else possible on this earth which you can say is more important than God? If not shouldn't God be your first and primary goal?

BELOVED, all things are possible with God, why don't you try to fit into his plan? Even you might surprise yourself, you wouldn't surprise Him.

HOW CAN PLAN

HOW CAN I FIND A PATH TO CLIMB
TAKING ME TO GOD?
HOW CAN I TAKE TIME TO PLAN
A POSSIBLE WINNING JOB?

HOW WILL I TELL EVERYONE
THAT I'VE STARTED ON THE WAY?
HOW CAN I BELIEVE ALL
THESE THINGS I SAY?
HOW CAN I FIND THE TIME I NEED
TO DO ALL SET BEFORE ME?
HOW CAN ANYONE BELIEVE
ALL THE WAYS THERE BE?
HOW CAN THERE COME ABOUT
A WINNING WAY FOREVER?
HOW CAN I KEEP BELIEVING
THIS IS A TRUE ENDEAVOR?

HOW CAN I FUND AND PAY
MAKING SURE THIS PLAN?
HOW CAN I, ALL ALONE
SUCCEED A MERE MAN?
HOW CAN I BE ALL I SHOULD
UNLESS GOD TAKES MY HAND?
HOW CAN I REACH OUT TO HEAVEN
NOT KNOWING WHERE I STAND?
HOW CAN I FIND HELP FROM GOD
WHERE IS THIS SURE CONNECTION?
HOW CAN I HOLD FATHER'S HAND
WITHOUT HIS CLEAR DIRECTION?
HOW CAN ALL THIS COME ABOUT
AND TAKE ME THROUGH TO HEAVEN?
HOW CAN I NOT BELIEVE IT'S
JESUS I'VE BEEN GIVEN?

BELOVED, how can I bring you all the good things I have for
you when you won't wait upon Me and listen for My voice? How
long must I ask for your whole heart, didn't I give you Mine? My
dear ones the time is disappearing rapidly and We have not yet

gathered all of the lost ones. Come let us be closer together and finish God's work.

BELOVED, every call from now on is most important. We must be about the Father's business. This last cleanup is most important. Can't you sense the urgency of the time?

THE CALL

THERE ARE MANY VOICES,
MAKING NOISY DEMANDS.
THERE ARE EAGER ONES RUNNING,
OBEYING MAN'S COMMANDS.
BUT SELDOM DO YOU HEAR RING OUT,
THE TRUTH MY CHILDREN SHOUT.

COME UNTO ME ALL YOU LOST,
LISTEN NOW AND WIN.
HEAR THE TRUTH THEY SHOUT ABOUT,
LEARN TO SHED YOUR SIN.
AND THEN YOU'LL KNOW MY PEACE,
AND FIND LIFE THAT WILL NOT CEASE.

LISTEN WELL WHILE ECHOES RING,
TELLING OF HEAVEN ABOVE.
HEAR THE SOUNDS OF LOVERS,
SINGING OF MY LOVE.
AND NEVER AGAIN FALL PREY,
COME INTO MY ARMS TO STAY.

HEAR MY CALL ON EARTH RIGHT NOW,
FORGET YOUR SELFISH WAY.
INVITE JESUS INTO YOUR HEART,
MAKE SURE IN HEAVEN YOU STAY.
GOD MADE FOR YOU A MANSION GREAT,
SHOWING HIS LOVE, SEALING YOUR FATE.

BELOVED, how can you have heaven as a sure place for you and not be concerned about all My children that still are without? Is My love so buried that you can't let it out? Come let us find a job that you can do for Me. Seek Me in the morning while I can still be found, listen and I will tell you of My plans.

DOUBT

WHAT IS REBELLION ALL ABOUT?
RIPPING, TEARING THROWING OUT,
FAKING TRUTH AND DISBELIEVING.
FINDING FAULT ALWAYS GRIEVING.
WHERE DO YOU GO WITH ALL YOUR DOUBT?

IS THERE JOY IN TEARING DOWN,
ACTING SMART BEING THE CLOWN?
DO YOU BUILD ANYTHING GOOD,
ARE YOU DOING WHAT YOU SHOULD?
WHERE WILL YOU GO WITH ALL YOUR DOUBT?

CAN YOUR RANTING, CRYING OUT,
BRING ANY GOOD WITH A SHOUT?
WHERE DO YOU FIND YOUR REWARD?
WITH TIRED PEOPLE YOU HAVE BORED?
WHERE WILL YOU GO WITH YOUR DOUBT?

COME TO JESUS RIGHT AWAY,
FIND THE SON, FIND A NEW DAY.
THE PEACE YOU HAVE BRINGS NEW LIFE,
STRESS IS GONE SO IS STRIFE.
NOW WHERE IS ALL THAT DOUBT?

BELOVED, there is no proof like the proof of Jesus in your heart, hidden and safe never to depart.

LET'S TALK

HOW OFTEN TROUBLE FLIES AWAY
WHEN EVERY PERSON HAS THEIR SAY,
UNDERSTANDING COMES THAT WAY.

EVERY PERSON SHOULD VENT THEIR RAGE
OR MAKE DISPLAY AS ON A STAGE,
CLEAN UP THEIR ACT, START A NEW PAGE.

THROUGH TALKING GOOD THINGS COME
JUST TRY AWHILE AN YOU'LL GET SOME,
JUST MAKE TALK A RULE OF THUMB.

SPEECH COMES IN MANY A FORM
SOME WILL HELP, OTHERS WILL HARM,
GOOD SPEECH WILL SHOW YOUR CHARM.

LEARN TO TALK SO OTHERS WILL HEAR
BY PROPER SPEECH MAKE LOVE APPEAR,
DO IT RIGHT AND ALL WILL CHEER.

TELL OF JESUS, TALK THAT WAY
AND YOU'LL FIND FRIENDS WILL STAY,
BRING YOU COMFORT, MAKE YOUR DAY.

NOW WILL YOU TALK SOME MORE
SHOW YOUR FRIENDS YOU'RE NOT A BORE?
LET EVERYONE KNOW TALK'S NO CHORE.

BELOVED, when things don't seem to be going your way have you ever thought you might need a change of direction? This thought is to cause you to stop and ask BY whom am I being led? Is self your prime motivator or is Jesus? My dear ones these are the times We should be very close together, you need Me now!

BELOVED, come close and We will talk, have you ever really done that with Me? These are the very last days, the end times, yes the closing of this age of the Gentiles, and it is to your great advantage to have My guidance. It is no idle suggestion when I say come let Us talk. Obedience, to obey, there is a word to pay attention to. Great riches and blessings are being held back because of lack of obedience

BELOVED, when every day is over it's like the end of time, something is finished, and it's left forever. Have you ever felt that the end of day is like the closing of a door? Have you just left a room you'll never visit again? You should take a different look at each day I give you and ask yourself if you could do it over would you do it better? My dear children this is why I ask you to bring Me into every day for I will lead and guide you to make the most of your days!

BELOVED, when days pass by and you feel I am not with you, never go by your feelings. Self and flesh will fool you for I will never leave you. These are My times of watching, waiting and observing how you are doing. How are you doing?

BELOVED, your days are worthless to you if you are just doing your "thing". You should always be doing My "things" now. These are your last chance growth periods don't blow it!

BELOVED, pay attention to My words they are life and life everlasting. Remember this that I say and become worthy doers.

A DOER

WHAT MOVES ONES HEART
TO BE A DOER,
ARE THERE MANY WAYS?

WHERE DOES ONE FIND
THE MOTIVATION,
TO MAKE USEFUL WAYS?

CAN THERE BE MORE
TO ME,
IF I CHANGE MY WAYS?

WHAT CAN MEAN
MOST TO ME,
TO HEAR GOD AND OBEY?

BELOVED, there is no end to My way once your foot is firmly planted on the path I have set; it's your drive that takes you farther yet.

BELOVED, never doubt, it will leave you out. A weak heart is lost at the start. Stir up your bones and make a run for Me. I will always be there to catch you.

WHAT MOVES YOU?

IS THERE A TOUCH STONE
IN YOUR HEAD,
A PLACE THAT TURNS YOU ON?

OR DOES THE BIBLE
WORDS OF TRUTH,
JUST EXCITE YOUR YAWN?

CAN GOD'S WORDS
MOTIVATE YOU, AND
CAUSE YOU TO GO ON?

SEEK MORE TRUTH
YES, DIG DEEPER,
READING UNTIL DAWN!

CAN WORDS CARE AND
DRAW YOU CLOSE,
EVER MOVING ON?

OR WILL YOU
JUST WIND UP
A LOST, AND LOSING JOHN?

BELOVED, listen, yes, learn to listen, listen in your heart, listen because you love, listen to learn. Listen to Me!

BELOVED, these short notes can bring long life with great rewards, but only when obeyed. Do you read and forget? Do you read and then not do? Do you read for amusement? Why are you now looking at these words? Why bother? My dear ones unless I stir your heart by words I put in your head nothing will work. What shall I say, moving you to start?

BELOVED, try and try again in all worthwhile endeavors for that is the will of the Lord for you. See everything I put before you as worthwhile, good or bad. My school of learning takes many a strange turn but you should always know where it comes from. BELOVED, work is to be a blessing, trials are to be a blessing; be blessed by circumstances for I have placed you there. Are you not mine? Have I not made you? Is My love not real? What do you believe I made you for? This is a reality check!

WHAT'S REAL?

ARE FLOWERS GRASS AND TREES
REAL AND LIVING ON?
ARE ROCKS AND SOIL, ALL EARTH
EXISTING NOW AND NEVER GONE?
WHAT HAPPENS TO WATER AND TO EARTH
AND WHERE GOES MAN FROM BIRTH?

WHAT IS THIS SPIRIT THING?
IS THERE A HEAVENLY PLACE?
WHAT IS UNSEEN AND WHERE,
WHAT REALLY IS IN SPACE?
WHAT HAPPENS AFTER LIFE
IS THERE AN END TO STRIFE?

WITHOUT A HOPE AHEAD,
WHAT WORTH IS LIFE TODAY?
IF ALL I SEE AND KNOW,
WILL QUICKLY GO AWAY?
DOES JESUS REALLY LIVE,
AND LIFE FOREVER GIVE?

BELOVED, learn and know the reality of this life I have put in each child. All are Mine all are precious to Me and all will have a true life everlasting who are willing to come as I call. Reality of life is what makes it worth living. Seek and find this truth, it is ever unfolding.

BELOVED, all is not quickly given or shown, told or explained, how could it be? The only believable explanation comes through the living of it. Training in truth and trust totally thrills the thinking ones. Your born-again Spirit is the open door to My everlasting life of loving wonders.

TRUTH REVEALED

THERE IS A LIFTING OF A VEIL
A PARTING OF THE WAY,
WHERE MAN CAN GROW IN LOVE
AND VIEW WHERE HE WILL STAY.

NEVER DOUBT, IT BLURS THE SIGHT
TO SEE YOU'LL NEVER KNOW,
FOR DOUBTING BUILDS A WALL
WHERE NOTHING EVER SHOWS.

SO HOW CAN TRUTH
BE TOLD RIGHT NOW,
WHEN YOU HAVE NO PAST
TO SHOW YOU HOW?

YOUR TRIP IS ONE OF FAITH
ONLY DOING TEACHES HOW,
IS ALL TRUTH MADE PLAIN
DO YOU UNDERSTAND IT NOW?

BELOVED, what can writing do right now to help people see truth? **Nothing** if they can't get the information. **Nothing** if the data is given to them and they don't read. **Nothing** if they read and don't do. So writing is worthless unless the work is received, read, rehearsed and practiced! The worth of books depends on the cooperation of many, writing only starts the chain of events required to make books of any use to the Father. So pray for a perfect circle of completion for book writing!

BELOVED, never can progress be made in any worthwhile endeavor until cooperation is received from all who need to participate. So pray for the Father to pull hearts together and make your work fruitful. Learn to see the overall job requirements, then pray for help in all sectors of endeavor.

TOGETHER

MAKE A PLAN AND EXECUTE
THE THINGS YOU KNOW TO DO.
NEVER ALLOW CONDEMNING DOUBT
IT KEEPS CONDEMNING YOU.

YOU NEED TO WORK TOGETHER
WITH TRUST AND FAITH IN HAND.
UNLESS THERE'S COOPERATION
YOU'LL NOT KNOW WHERE YOU STAND.

NOW WHO SHOULD BE YOUR PARTNERS?
WHAT WILL WORK THE BEST?
NEVER LEAVE OUT LOVE
AND ALWAYS USE THIS TEST.

ARE YOU FEELING CONFIDENT
IN WHAT YOU'RE LED TO DO?
BEING CLOSE TOGETHER
WILL ALWAYS SEE YOU THROUGH.

NOW TOGETHER MEANS WITH SOMEONE
WHO KNOWS AS MUCH AS YOU.
TOGETHER SHOULD SHOW TRUST
IN EVERYTHING YOU DO.

ASK THE FATHER TO ASSIST
WITH JESUS HOLD HIS HAND.
USE THE HOLY SPIRIT AND
YOU'LL CONQUER ALL THE LAND.

BELOVED, to know to do and do not turns out to be a waste, if you believe this make every effort to follow through each task by asking the Father for help. Why do you find it so difficult to come to the Father and talk over your problems? **Have a close encounter of the trusting kind.** You'll never know what you're missing until you believe.

BELOVED, when your body tires you must consider it. Learn to rest and pace yourself. The Father gives you the body as a gift and it is to be used to worship the Father and enjoy all His provisions for you.

BELOVED, the living of life that I desire for you will prove to be the life you would chose if self weren't driving you to meet its demands. I had to provide you a freedom of choice so I could trust you when I open eternity and invite you in. So treat your body with the respect due it and it will transport you into realms of wonder not yet released!

REALMS OF WONDER

WHERE WILL I TAKE YOU HOW CAN YOU KNOW?
UNLESS YOU'RE PATIENT AND LET ME SHOW.
MY REVELATION OF WONDERS DISPLAYED,
WILL ONLY OCCUR AFTER I'VE MADE,
A THOROUGH TESTING OF PEOPLE THROUGH TIME.

YOUR PATIENCE WILL CARRY YOU THROUGH
TUNNELS OF TIME AND THINGS YOU'LL DO.
ALL THE WHILE GROWING IN SPIRIT'S PLACE,
AS I KEEP YOU MOVING IN SPACE,
YOU'LL FIND JOY AND RHYTHM AND RHYME.

WITHOUT A DOUBT IS YOUR WAY TO GROW,
KEEPING YOUR TRUST SO I'LL ALWAYS KNOW.
JUST HOW YOU'RE DOING, KEEP DOING YOUR BEST,
YOU'LL ALWAYS BE TREATED AS MY GUEST,
AS I TAKE YOU ON YOUR DAILY CLIMB.

THE HEAVENS ABOVE WILL PROVE A GREAT TEST,
BUT THROUGH IT ALL YOU'LL SHOW YOUR BEST.
DELIGHTS ABOVE AND WONDERS BELOW,
YOU'LL BE BLESSED WHEREVER YOU GO,
MY LOVE WILL ENFOLD YOU MY LOVE DEVINE.

BELOVED, keep your eyes always on the goal I have for you "Oneness" with Me. Bury it in your heart, sew it to your soul, bind it on your path with believing the only way. Seek to know with growing certainty how much I love you and how much it's really worth to you.

BELOVED, believe you have already love enough to see through whatever comes your way and I'll always give you more. Become My vessels of love and watch how fast you will grow. The few years ahead of you will prove to be the fastest growth time I've yet allowed. It only happens to those who grab and run with the gifts I give.

BELOVED, now can you stop all of your thinking about the past? Now can you just think about what We can do together? Do not look back on your failures or disappointments just look ahead at the victory We are about to have. You will never get where I want to take you looking back, I don't! You shouldn't either.

BELOVED, My love never fails you, My love is always right there for you, are you always right there with My love? Remember no matter what, I am there for you. Not by sight, sound or feel do you depend, but on My Word.

BELOVED, the simple act of trust is all I ask; do you trust Me in all things, everywhere all the time? Faith and trust, believe and know, put them on like boots and always walk in them, for they will keep your feet on the true path.

TRUE PATH

THERE IS A WAY GIVEN TO MAN
THAT SEEMS SO SURE AND GOOD,
JUST WHERE IT GOES HE SHOULD ASK
JUST TO BE SURE, HE SHOULD.

NEVER ACCEPT THE EASY WAY
IT MIGHT NOT BE SO GOOD,
DON'T JUST GO RIGHT AHEAD
JUST BECAUSE YOU COULD.

THE RIGHT WAY MAY SEEM WRONG
ITS PATHWAY MAY BE HARD,
THE GOOD WAY SEEMS TOUGH
APPEARING TO BE BARRED.

WHY IS THIS WAY SO RIGHT?
I'M BECOMING SCARRED.
HURT AND PAIN MY REWARD
HAVING TROUBLE FROM THE START.

WHEN I CALL FOR YOU TO HELP?
YOUR HELP IS ALWAYS THERE.
THEN I KNOW, YOUR WAY I GO
TRAVELING UP HEAVEN'S STAIRS.

BELOVED, the easy way seems simple and best, but you'll never reach heaven without the test. Trust is a must if you would leave trouble in the dust.

BELOVED, will My love ever cease? Will the earth and heavens and all My universe go away? Will Never ever happen?

BELOVED, just think about the wonders I've already given to you. Jesus came in the flesh, Jesus buried your sins, and Jesus gave you the Holy Spirit. Jesus gave you everlasting life. Jesus cleansed you of sin and Jesus loves you. Wouldn't that be enough to prove Our love? Now what will your love do for Us and with Us?

BELOVED, how can I bring to you the way you must go when you don't accept the why you should go? Don't you yet know why you should do everything I ask and why you should make Me your only goal. Do you know why you should be My witnesses, why you should give Me your life so I can give you Mine?

BELOVED, never belittle who you are. Who you are, what you are, why you are is all summed up in "A gift of God to Himself". Take this thought and make it a driving force of will to be all that you can be just for Him who made and loves you!

SHARE SEVEN

THE GIFT

GOD WRAPPED A GIFT
IN THE FLESH OF MAN,
HE GAVE US HIS SON
TO SHOW THAT HE CAN,
GIVE UP HIMSELF
AS A GIFT OF LOVE.

HE SUFFERED OUR SIN
TO MAKE US SIN FREE,
CARRIED SICKNESS IN FLESH
THEN DIED ON A TREE,
HE GAVE UP HIMSELF
AS A GIFT OF LOVE.

NOW CAN YOU GIVE
A GIFT IN RETURN?
CAN YOU GIVE UP SELF
AS A WAY TO EARN,
THAT GIFT OF LOVE
WHEN HE GAVE HIMSELF?

BELOVED, you should think more highly of yourself just because of your potential. If you only could understand what the Father has in His mind for you, more reason to love one another.

BELOVED, when great moves of Mine take place they have small beginnings. I start in an insignificant way. It's the slow, steady growth that will bring lasting results. Never judge My works by how they start, remember Jesus!

BELOVED, always make your growth sure and steady before trying to help someone else. Blind leading the blind doesn't work!

BELOVED, spend more time in prayer and more time talking with Me and listening to Me. What kind of a relationship do We have when this isn't happening? What kind of a relationship will We have if We are closer?

BELOVED, try a little harder, try to witness a little more, pray a little more, wait upon Me a little more, please try a little more. Just a little more!

YOUR TIME

WHERE DOES YOUR TIME GO?
WHERE DOES IT ALL COME FROM?
WHAT IS IT REALLY FOR?
WHY DO YOU STILL HAVE SOME?

IS YOUR TIME REALLY YOURS?
WHO CAN IT BE BORROWED FROM?
DO YOU EVER HAVE ENOUGH?
DO YOU ALWAYS WANT SOME?

WILL YOU EVER USE TIME UP?
IS THERE TIME YOU RUN FROM?
CAN YOU MAKE TIME SLOW DOWN?
AND SAVE IT 'TILL YOU WANT SOME?

WHEN YOUR END OF TIME COMES,
WILL OTHERS KNOW YOUR PAST?
HAVE YOU LEFT A TRAIL BEHIND,
OF BLESSINGS THAT WILL LAST?

DO YOU KNOW WHAT'S NEXT?
WHAT REWARD COMES FROM YOUR PAST?
WILL YOU BE HAPPY LOOKING BACK?
SEEING A LIFE AHEAD AT LAST?

BELOVED, use your time to build a life ahead for others, then your reward will be made sure!

BELOVED, look for Me by your side, talk with Me as you go, bring Me along now and you shall have Me always. We are One now if you will only receive, act and believe!

ONE

THE MIND OF MAN IS SLOW,
TO RECEIVE THE WILL TO KNOW,
ABOUT THE THINGS I SHOW,
SO HE, WITH ME, MAY GO.

TO BE ONE WITH ME NOW,
IS WHAT I WILL ALLOW,
WHY DO YOU ASK HOW,
WHEN I'M BEHIND THE PLOW?

BELOVED, do not doubt when I say things you don't understand, believe and receive by asking. Are you not mine called to be in My image? That means just what it says yet you still have doubts. Don't harbor unbelief it will steal from you all I plan.

BELOVED, I am not calling you to walk along a glory path of ease, I'm calling you to come and follow Me. Don't you trust and believe?

TRUST AND BELIEVE

ALL I EVER ASK,
ALL I EVER HOPE,
ALL I EVER DESIRE,
IS IN MY CHILDREN.
JUST TRUST AND BELIEVE!

ALL YOU EVER RECEIVE,
ALL YOU CAN BELIEVE,
ALL I GIVE TO YOU,
IS ALL YOU'LL EVER NEED.
JUST TRUST AND BELIEVE!

ALL THE FATHER'S DESIRE,
ALL THAT WILL TRANSPIRE,
ALL YOUR WAY IS PLANNED,
THAT'S WHERE YOU'LL ALWAYS BE,
JUST TRUST AND BELIEVE!

BELOVED, it is not what you imagine, not what you dream up, it is not what you desire, it is not how you can understand, it is only what I planned, that lies ahead for you, just trust and believe it's greater than you can conceive!

BELOVED, love knows no boundaries, knows no restraints, and has no walls or fences about it; love true love is free! Just relax, you are in good hands, forever. It is Our eternity that the Father releases. Your part is to stay the course, stick in there, carry on, keep on keeping on, never doubt, never quit and you'll never fail!

TO FAIL

FAILURE IS NOT A WAY,
FAILURE IS NEVER PLANNED,
FAILURE ONLY REFLECTS,
THE UNBELIEF OF MAN.

TO FAIL BEGINS WITH DOUBT,
THEN TROUBLE ROUNDS IT OUT.
WHILE MORE HARM DEVELOPS,
YOU JUST SCREAM AND SHOUT!

NOW FAILURE BRINGS IN SIN,
AND SIN WILL TEAR APART,
NOW TERROR HAS JUST ENTERED,
HOW DID ALL THIS START?

YOU DIDN'T CALL ON ME,
YOU TURNED AND LEFT ME OUT,
NOW YOU HAVE BEFORE YOU,
THE RESULTS OF SIN AND DOUBT.

YOU CANNOT GO ALONE,
YOU WILL BE ATTACKED,
YOU ARE NOT ABLE,
WITHOUT ME AT YOUR BACK.

TO FAIL IS NOT MY PLAN,
TO FAIL IS ON YOUR OWN,
YOU CAN FAIL ALONE,
OR DO WHAT I HAVE SHOWN!

BRING ME ALONG EACH DAY,
THEN FAILURE IS NOT YOUR WAY,
COME INTO MY ARMS,
THAT IS WHERE TO STAY!

BELOVED, what can one man alone do to help people? What can one man alone do to help himself? Why would one man be alone? My children are never alone some of them just think they are, why?

BELOVED, always call on Me, reach for Me, early in the morning, I am always there for you. When you call then We can fellowship and plan your day. Just taking the time with Me can make your day so much more pleasant. Learn to set a goal. This is the best way to begin My plan for you. I allow your plan for you but just where has that taken you in the past?

YOUR WAY

HAVE YOU EVER PLANNED YOUR WAY
AND FOUND THINGS DIDN'T WORK?
HAVE YOU HAD EXPERIENCES
MAKING YOU OUT A JERK?

WHY CONTINUE PUSHING
TO GET EVERYTHING YOUR WAY?
JUST GIVE UP INDEPENDENCE
ASK ME TO HELP AND STAY.

MY WAY FOR YOU IS SET
I'VE GIVEN YOU MUCH THOUGHT.
YOUR PATH WILL CAUSE YOUR GROWTH
IN AREAS LONG SOUGHT.

ALL THIS IS BOUND TO HAPPEN
WHEN YOUR WAY BECOMES ALL MINE.
NOW YOU'LL HAVE THE BLESSING
YOUR WAY COULDN'T FIND!

BELOVED, never believe that you have to do it all alone, when you are Mine you are always One with Me, the Father and all Our Family. You must try to live as part of Us not by yourself any longer. Call out to Me I will answer, but it must be in true desire believing!

BELOVED, find the true life, the one I have planned for you. These are the last days for My children to grow into My place for you and receive all the Father has for you. Your obedience now can make Jesus' judgment time such a wonderful happy time of rejoicing. I am opening your moments now to become accelerated times of obedience with Spirit growth of wonders. Let's talk!

TALKING

MAKE TALKING TOGETHER
A TIME OF TRUE BONDING,
FORGET IDLE TALK LIKE WEATHER.

TRUE TALK HAS POWER TO BRING
ALL HEAVEN TO EARTH,
CAUSING EVERYONE TO SING.

NOW TURN ALL YOUR TALK
TO LOVE, PEACE AND JOY,
THEN SING WHILE YOU WALK.

LET TALKING FLOW FREE
LET LOVE BE ITS SOURCE,
JUST SEE WHAT CAN BE.

BELOVED, each morning when you wake up start to think of Jesus. Welcome Him into your day and invite Him to share your time. Ask Him to help you and lead you into a beautiful walk into the day He has planned for you. Believe and receive what He wants to show you.

BELOVED, this is the true walk for My children; the walk with Jesus. This is the true talk; the talk with Jesus. This is the true life; the life with Jesus. Won't you begin this life today?

NEW LIFE

HOW CAN YOU KNOW MY LOVE?
IF YOU WON'T RECEIVE MY PLAN,
HOW CAN I SHOW MY LOVE,
UNLESS YOU SEE I CAN?

START A NEW LIFE TODAY,
BY GIVING UP THE PAST.
MAKE A NEW LIFE SO REAL,
YOU KNOW THAT IT WILL LAST.

NEW LIFE HAS BEEN MY DREAM,
THE ONE LONG PLANNED FOR YOU.
I'VE WAITED UNTIL NOW,
TO SEE WHAT YOU WOULD DO.

NEW LIFE BEGINS FOREVER ,
AS TIME IS PUT BEHIND.
OBEY MY WORDS I TELL YOU,
AND ETERNITY YOU'LL FIND.

BELOVED, I am trying every way I can to reach you and bring you into the fullness of life right now. These are the very end times for you, then these earth life opportunities vanish. A whole new way unfolds. Your   spurt growth now gains you greater position and place with Me. Be obedient draw closer than ever imagined possible, I will help.

BELOVED, hesitation and doubt are becoming very costly for you to continue entertaining them.

BELOVED, just start the morning by inviting Me to be with you all day, then act as if I were! I am anyway but you hardly ever talk with Me. Make Me your dear friend.

A FRIEND SO DEAR

CAN YOU FIND A FRIEND SO DEAR,
WHO'S ALWAYS BY YOUR SIDE?
WHY HAVE YOU NEVER REALIZED,
THE PLACE WHERE I ABIDE?

RIGHT IN YOUR HEART
I STAY ALL DAY,
THROUGH THE NIGHT BESIDE.

A FRIEND WHO HELPS,
AND YOU DON'T KNOW.
ONE YOU SEEM UNSURE,
JUST HOW FAR HE'LL GO.

RIGHT IN YOUR HEART
I STAY ALL DAY,
THROUGH THE NIGHT YOU KNOW.

SO DRAW CLOSER IN BELIEF,
RIGHT NOW AND YOU'LL FIND.
THE TIME I'LL SPEND,
JUST TO MAKE YOU MINE!

RIGHT IN YOUR HEART
I STAY FOREVER,
I'M THE STAYING KIND.

BELOVED, your growth occurs as I release to you patterns and methods that you obey. No other effort on your part means so much. Open your understanding to receive more from Me. As you grow in obedience I release more. Love is the oil of growth fueling the flames warming the hearts of the lost.

BELOVED, see yourself as resting in the hands of love, see love slowly kneading and working out the blemishes and then adding growth ingredients required for perfection. Submission increases expansion in all areas. Obedience to do all you know you should do will bring more "know you should dos".

WHAT TO DO?

HOW CAN I TELL JUST WHAT TO DO
WHEN THE WORLD CALLS OUT SO LOUD?
HOW WILL I KEEP ON LOVE'S PATH
IF I KEEP FOLLOWING THE CROWD?

I CALL RIGHT NOW TO FATHER GOD
REQUESTING YOUR GUIDANCE AND CARE,
BUT HOW CAN I EVER BE SURE
THAT YOU'RE ALWAYS THERE?

DOES THE BIBLE SAY WHAT TO DO?
CAN I FIND ANSWERS RIGHT NOW?
WHEN CAN I GO AND WHO TO ASK?
IS THERE ANYONE TO TELL ME HOW?

AGREEMENT

DO YOU FIND AGREEMENT
AMONG ALL YOUR FRIENDS AROUND?
CAN THERE BE COMPATABILITY
CAN IT REALLY BE FOUND?

HARMONY AND FRIENDSHIP
SEEMS MOST DIFFICULT TO FIND.
I'VE SEARCHED AROUND THE WORLD
AND NEVER FOUND THAT KIND.

THERE'S ALWAYS TROUBLE AND UPSET
THERE SEEMS TO BE A LOT.
WHEN CAN I EVER FIND
THE HARMONY MOST SOUGHT?

DOES THIS SOUND LIKE YOU
MAY HAVE WALKED THIS WAY?
LET ME BRING YOU HELP
LISTEN TO WHAT I SAY.

IN JESUS THERE IS HARMONY
IN JESUS YOU'LL FIND LOVE.
THROUGH JESUS COMES THE ANSWER
STRAIGHT FROM FATHER ABOVE.

ASK JESUS TO COME AND ABIDE
ASK HIM TO SAVE YOU NOW.
JUST SAY MY LORD I NEED YOU
THE BIBLE WILL TELL YOU HOW?

BELOVED, your walk daily only needs to have Me leading and guiding, however I never just take over and do that. We must be so close and so well tuned to each other that your walk is MY walk because Our walk is in loving accord.

BELOVED. All of these words all of these writings are just meaningless ink and paper without your heart touching My heart in "hearty" agreement.

SHARE EIGHT

BELOVED, try, try and keep on trying to be more like Jesus. How, how can that be? Just be obedient to the things I tell you and then I can do the work. Give up self and selfish ways seek to hear from Me. There that's your start. Read your Bible; be hungry for the word and I will see that you are satisfied.

BELOVED, just give Me more time you don't have much longer to do that! Will you wake up right now and be a doer for Me? All these little notes I've given you are your pathways to Oneness, why aren't you more excited about this?

A FATHER'S DREAM

A CHILD RECEIVED FROM GOD ABOVE
A GIFT GIVEN FROM THE HEART OF LOVE.

HOW CAN THIS BE SUCH A GIFT TO ME?
MY WIFE FROM GOD GIVES A CHILD I SEE.

HE GROWS AND BUILDS A LIFE ALONE
HE'S OUT OF TOUCH WHAT HAVE I SOWN?

I TRAINED AND TAUGHT ALL THAT I KNOW
I GAVE HIM JESUS, JESUS I TRIED TO SHOW.

MY DREAM FOR HIM HAS DISAPPEARED
AND WHAT I HAVE IS SOMETHING WEIRD!

THE WORLD HAS CLAIMED THAT CHILD OF MINE
BUT I ASKED JESUS MY BOY TO FIND.

AND JESUS SAVED, MY DREAM CAME TRUE
I DEPENDED ON JESUS, MY DREAM TO DO.

BELOVED, always turn to Me, call on Me early in the morning. Let's plan your day and I will keep you on the path of rapid growth, rapid growth because you have waited so long to come to Me that We must hurry to bring you where you belong.

BELOVED, to pay attention to what you are reading and to do as instructed will bring you onto your path God has planned for you. Now is the time you are to be used to bring in the lost. Support Jesus' outreach around the world NOW. The time is short and you are dragging your feet. NOW is the time to get up and run! Do all you know to do then I will give you more!

FATE

THERE IS NO HURRY UP AND WAIT
IF YOU JUST LIE THERE THAT'S YOUR FATE!

JUST BE STEADY GET UP AND GO
I'LL PUT YOU ON A PATH YOU KNOW.

TURN YOUR TIME OVER TO ME
AND GET A FATE YOU'LL WANT TO SEE.

TELL ABOUT JESUS, TELL THE LOST
EXPLAIN WHAT DISOBEDIENCE COSTS.

HELL AND HEAVEN, MAKE THEM REAL
TELL THE LOST OF A LOVE THEY'LL FEEL!

SHOW FATE AS A GOLDEN ROOM
SAVE THE LOST FROM THEIR DOOM.

BELOVED, listen as never before these times are real, My time is coming to welcome My Bride. There is a joy in heaven that's hard to hide. We all want to shout and sing, "Here comes the Bride". Do not slack now but rise up, be cleansed and made whole.

See the truth leap out to you as you read the Bible. I'll use all I am able to do to hasten Our meeting in the air. Do not later look back and say why wasn't I more obedient, but use this catch-up time to hasten you to your proper place with Me!

BELOVED, when dusk falls, when darkness begins everyone who can starts turning on lights. Well darkness is descending and the time to turn on the lights is NOW! The light of the world must shine through the hearts and lives of all the saved ones. Show NOW your loyalty, NOW your trust, and NOW your worth to the Father. Rise up where you are and be led by your Holy Spirit as never before. I am with you leading and guiding all of the WAY.

BELOVED, many are not able or just won't listen to the Father, so those who do are doubly burdened, but that is not bad, they shall be doubly blessed. Rise early, listen, learn, obey and go!

BELOVED, take these small "beloveds" as pills of healing, first for your healing then for the healing of the lost. Right now, right where you are, is the place and now is the time to move as never before doing the work of the kingdom.

KINGDOM WORK

THERE WAS A KING WHO HAD EVERYTHING
HE SEARCHED FOR MORE TO DO.

HE ASKED REAL NICE AND SOUGHT ADVICE
AND WONDERED WHO WOULD COME THROUGH.

BUT THROUGHOUT HIS LAND NONE TOOK A STAND
THE KING PERPLEXED DIDN'T HAVE A CLUE.

WITH LOVE HE SOUGHT FOR WHAT HE BOUGHT
LOVE COVERED HIS LAND LIKE DEW.

AND THEN THIS LOVE SENT FROM ABOVE
BECAME THE KING'S WORK CREW.

HIS WORK OF LOVE SPREAD HEART TO HEAD
AND THE ENTIRE KINGDOM GREW!

BELOVED, you must believe to receive. It must come from My heart to your heart. Let My love be so real that your acceptance is quick and true. Be open and seeking as never before because I am giving more than has ever been released in the past. This is the closing of an age. This is the end of one great endeavor and favor and blessings are about to flow. My listening obedient ones are to be first and most blessed!

BELOVED, can the dreams of man become real? Yes man has been given great power and ability to create on this earth. In his own strength man can organize and control vast empires. How much more can a man do if My Spirit leads him? The problem is will man pursue his own dream or will he seek Mine? The great things We will do together will be My way not man's way. Are you ready to give up your way and follow My way?

BELOVED, if your enthusiasm was directed toward My plan

and Me, then your enthusiasm would take you to great heights in My kingdom. My dear one it is the self driving you when you still long for your way.

MY WAY

WHEN I SEE A CHALLENGE I WILL TAKE IT ON
BECAUSE I CAN DISPLAY HOW I'M NEVER WRONG.
I'M SMART ENOUGH TO WIN EVERY GAME I PLAY
WHY IS IT NO ONE SEEMS TO LIKE MY WAY?

MY WAY MAKES ME HAPPY MOST OF THE TIME
SOMETIMES MY WINNING SEEMS LIKE A CRIME.
OTHERS SEEM TO THINK MY WAY IS WRONG
MY WAY IS WINNING I KNOW WHERE I BELONG.

I WAS IN THE WINNER'S SEAT WHEN DISASTER CAME
ALL MY DREAMS JUST VANISHED,
I'M NOT THE SAME.
MY HEALTH HAS FAILED I CAN'T HOLD UP MY HEAD
MY MEMORY IS FADING I DON'T KNOW
WHAT I SAID.

NOW MY WAY IS LONELY I CAN FIND NO REST
I'M WONDERING WAS MY WAY REALLY BEST?
I'VE HEARD TALK OF JESUS SOME GUY WITH LOVE
I MIGHT GIVE HIM A TRY IF I GET A SHOVE.

BELOVED, you should never be alone, when you give yourself to Me We become One. I am always with you but you have to accept and acknowledge Me and invite Me into your life. I do not take you over We become brothers and family in all We do.

BELOVED, if you will just draw closer to Me now you will find a rapid growth possible. I will help you become what the Father has always planned for you. Yes, He has always had great plans for you. Only doubt keeps you out, believe and receive.

BELIEVE

TO BELIEVE IN WHAT, BELIEVE WHO
MEANS TO BE CAREFULL IN WHAT YOU DO.
ASK FOR GUIDANCE SEEK HELP ALONG THE WAY
AND YOU WILL FIND A PLEASANT PLACE TO STAY.

TO BELIEVE IN SELF AND YOUR STRONG ARM
WILL LEAD YOU ASTRAY WILL CAUSE YOU HARM.
BELIEVE IN JESUS FOLLOW HIS LEAD
YOU WILL FIND OUT HOW TO SUCCEED!

THE BIBLE HAS PLANS, SHOWS YOU DIRECTION
KEEPS YOU FROM HARM REQUIRING CORRECTION.
WITH YOUR BIBLE IN HAND AND JESUS IN YOUR
HEART
BELIEVING IN GOD WILL BE A GREAT START!

BELOVED, to keep your life on an even keel you must balance work and play. Work is good and necessary you should pursue it with passion and purpose. To properly support the work, you care for your body with proper food and rest. Just as you plan and pursue work so should you consider play, what is play? True play is a release I give to you relieving stress and tension. Your proper play should bring fun, laughter and joy into your life and the life of the ones around you. The life I would have you lead is one of balance and happy growth. Do you experience any of these things?

BELOVED, when you plan to follow My lead you will find work, pleasure, fun and joy flowing quietly and peaceably. Why do you always imagine I only want to make you do Bible reading and church work? All of My asking you to read your Bible, seek Me in prayer etc. has been to bring you to a happy life.

A HAPPY LIFE

WHERE DO YOU FIND TRUE HAPPINESS?
IS IT HERE OR THERE BASED ON A GUESS?
NO MY CHILD IT'S IN MY ARMS
COME LISTEN CLOSE, KNOW MY CHARMS.

WHEN MY CHILDREN DO WHAT I SHOW
THEN ALL THEIR LIFE WITH ME THEY GO.
WE FIND TRUE PEACE AND GLADNESS EMPLOY,
THERE'S SINGING AND LAUGHTER FILLED WITH JOY.

EVENTS AND THRILLS AND GAMES WE PLAY
MAKING NEW FRIENDS ALONG THE WAY.
THIS IS LIFE THE WAY IT SHOULD BE
EXPRESSING LOVE ETERNALLY.
LIVING A HAPPY LIFE WITH ME.

BELOVED, how can you resist the gift of love that promises eternal freedom from fears, frustrations and fatality. Tell others about Jesus.

BELOVED, many are My little nudges and quite often I do push; it's all because of time, it's fast running out. Watch the clock not the calendar!

TIME

TIME IS FAST, TIME IS SLOW.
WHERE THE HECK DOES ALL TIME GO?
CAN YOU TELL TIME, TELL IT WHAT?
IT SEEMS IT'S JUST WHAT I THOUGHT.

I HAVE HOURS, MINUTES AND SECONDS,
WHERE THEY GO NO MAN RECKONS.
WHO STARTED TIME, CAN HE STOP IT?
DID HE PICK IT UP THEN JUST DROP IT?

DOES TIME END WHERE IS THAT?
IF YOU KNOW, THEN LET'S CHAT.
IF THERE IS UP AND THERE'S DOWN,
IF TIME STARTED, CAN THAT BE FOUND?

ALL THESE QUESTIONS ARE USING TIME,
I'M HARD PRESSED TO MAKE THIS RHYME.
SO BEAR WITH ME ONE MORE SECOND,
I'VE COME TO MY END TIME I RECKON!

BELOVED, do you have time for a happy life? Do you see yourself free from strife? You should know by now how to be an overcomer. You should be well on the way I have planned for you, are you?

BELOVED, always seek MY guidance not just every day but every hour, every minute. That is how close We need to be. Stop and think about the "catching away" not some time far off but in your Very Near Future, can you live with that, why not? You can't live without it!

CATCHING AWAY

HOW QUICK AND FAST THE CLOUDS CAPTURE
MY LOVE ONES IN THE RAPTURE.
NO MAN SHOULD BE ABSENT, MANY WILL,
KEEP TELLING OTHERS UNTIL I SAY BE STILL.

IN HEAVEN FATHER'S WAITING, ANGELS ARE AGLOW
WAITING FOR MY GLORY, MY BRIDE TO SHOW.
MILLIONS AND MILLIONS COMING TO THIS END
SHOWING THE FATHER'S LOVE AS
ANGELS DESCEND.

HEAVEN'S GREETINGS OUT OF CLOUDS OF LOVE
NOW THE GLORY COVERS EVERYONE ABOVE.
CHILDREN ALL AGLOW FILLED WITH
GLORIES' CHARM
NOW FOREVER SAVED FROM ALL EARTH'S HARM.

BELOVED, today something new something different something to make men think about where they are in truth and reality. In truth do you right now believe you're doing all you know you should be doing for the Father? Why don't you sit down and list five of the most important things you should be doing for the Father. Now put some time and dates to those five things. Now set your mind to follow your heart!

BELOVED, think about how to witness for Jesus You could just write some letters, you could take time, a set time each day, just to pray for the lost ones you know. You could just use the telephone, or you could pray and ask the Father to show you new people to phone, write to and speak to about Jesus.

THE WAYS OF LOVE

FOLLOW THE EASY PATH OF LOVE
ALL WORK WILL TAKE TIME AND PRAYER.
BE LED EACH HOUR BY HEAD AND HEART
NOW JESUS IS ABLE TO TAKE YOU THERE.

FOLLOW LOVE IT GUIDES WITH CARE
LOVE ALWAYS FOLLOWS HEART'S LEAD.
JUST KEEP YOUR EYES ON LOVE'S WAY
YOUR WORK FOR JESUS WILL SUCCEED.

WHERE LOVE GOES YOU FOLLOW IN TRUST
THE LORD ALWAYS MAKES PROVISION.
YOU'LL FIND GREAT JOY WITH EXPECTATION
WHEN YOU'RE MAKING THE RIGHT DECISION.

YES WAYS OF LOVE FLOW EASILY
YOU MOVE ON WINGS OF PRAYER.
KEEP LOVE IN SIGHT ALL THE TIME
YOU'LL FIND JESUS ALREADY THERE.

BELOVED, when Jesus calls you should always hear and answer. It is most important for you to be practicing now to hear Him. Listen, listen in the morning, listen at noon this is the "always path" to success.

BELOVED, quit procrastinating about your obedience once you start with Jesus you really have no way to turn, slow down, stop or quit!

BELOVED, Is there a heaven that is real to you? Well then how are you going to get there? Have you really started or are you still dragging your feet? Move man, get on God's Plan.

BELOVED, how can you do everything but follow Jesus? Now dear ones now is the GO time. If you have been reading this far you must know "GO", GO into the entire world!

YOUR WAY

WHAT WAY WILL YOU FIND TO GO?
WHAT PLACE IS CALLING YOU?
WHAT WAY DO YOU REALLY KNOW?
WHAT WORK CAN YOU REALLY DO?
ISN'T IT TIME TO MAKE DECISIONS?

WHAT REALLY TUGS AT YOUR HEART?
WHERE CAN YOU FIND RELIEF?
WHAT WAY IS YOURS TO START?
WHEN WILL YOU TEST YOUR BELIEF?
ISN'T IT TIME TO MAKE DECISIONS?

IS YOUR WAY ALL CUT AND DRIED
OR HAVE YOU LOST YOUR WAY?
MAYBE YOU NEED NEW DIRECTIONS
TO FIND A BETTER PLACE TO PLAY?
ISN'T IT TIME TO MAKE DECISIONS?

HAVE YOU A WAY THAT'S WORKING?
HAVE YOU FOUND REAL SATISFACTION?
HAS YOUR WAY BEEN PROVED OKAY?
DO YOU GET POSITIVE REACTION?
ISN'T IT TIME TO CHECK YOUR WAY?

WORD AND WAY

HEAR MY WORD AND FOLLOW IT
AND YOU'LL BE ON MY WAY.
LISTEN CAREFULLY, WISDOM GET
TO LIVE EACH HAPPY DAY.

HEAR MY WORD GO MY WAY
YOU'LL KNOW LOVE IS YOURS.
WORLDLY WAYS WILL BOW TO YOU
WHILE BLESSINGS WILL OCCUR.

HEAR MY WORD AND OBEY
AS OBEDIENCE CLEARS YOUR PATH.
YOU'LL FIND THAT DISCIPLINE
WILL KEEP AWAY MY WRATH.

HEAR MY WORD WALK MY WAY
FIND MANY LOST ARE SAVED.
YOU'LL BLESS OTHERS AS YOU RECEIVE
ALL THE THINGS YOU CRAVE.

BELOVED, make every day worthwhile by doing the things I ask you to do. Are you listening? I do not speak through or over or in a turmoil, or in a disquieting place. Set yourself apart and wait upon Me. In My presence you will find what you need.

BELOVED, keep your eyes on Spiritual, Heavenly goals and I will work out your earthly ones. Have confidence in My word and way then you will know peace and prosperity.

SHARE NINE

BELOVED, can you truly let go self and take on Jesus? Not by yourself! We must work closely together to bring about your miracle change, be assured that is what will happen. See the plan, capture the vision then live the change!

BELOVED, you make Me happy when you are consistent about returning to Me each morning. I will never fail you as you build your faith walk with Me.

BELOVED, it is so important that you be consistent in seeking. Willing hearts with willing hands become a useful tool of blessings to others and more to themselves as well.

HEAD AND HEART

TO MAKE A REAL IMPRESSION
HAVE A CONSISTENT CONFESSION,
LET YOUR HEART LEAD YOUR HEAD
AND BLESSINGS YOU'LL BE FED.

YOU SEE THERE LIES REAL TRUTH
FROM YOUR HEART WILL COME PROOF.
OF WHAT YOU'RE MADE TO BE
FOR ALL THE WORLD TO SEE.

IF IN YOUR HEAD YOU KNOW
IT'LL BE YOUR HEART YOU SHOW.
SO TAKE YOUR LEAD FROM ME
GREAT THINGS YOU SHALL SEE.

RECEIVE THE HEART FROM HEAVEN
USING TRUTH AS THE LEAVEN.
SHOW FORTH MY LOVE TO ALL
SAVE MANY FROM THE FALL.

LET THE HEAD TELL JESUS SAVES
SETTING FREE SATAN'S SLAVES.
AND WITH THE HEART SHOW LOVE
SPREADING BLESSING FROM ABOVE.

BELOVED, all of My children are given equal opportunities
and chances to grow as I lead. How few ever listen and pay attention. Where do you stand? Are you a hearer only? DO YOU DO?
BELOVED, every small step you take toward Me I take two
toward you. Why don't We meet more? Are you truly seeking more
of Me? Then do as I say, of course you'll have to be listening!

LISTENING EAR

A LISTENING EAR REQUIRES A CARING HEART
YOU MUST HAVE BOTH TO MAKE A START.
RISE EARLY LISTENING AND THEN YOU'LL BE
GROWING FAST IN LOVE, CONSTANTLY.

A LOVING EAR WILL STAY WELL TUNED
I'LL KEEP SUCH A ONE FROM FEAR, IMMUNE.
MY PROTECTION IS SAFE AND SECURE
ATTACKS AND TROUBLE YOU'LL NOT ENDURE.

A LISTENING EAR CAN KEEP YOU WELL,
A LOVING HEART ENHANCES THE SPELL.
SO TUNE YOUR EAR TO BE A BLESSING
WE'LL KEEP THE EVIL ONES A'GUESSING!

BELOVED, it is, as you believe you receive so build your trust
in Me by reading your Bible more, seek My face, have a listening
ear.
BELOVED, help is always right by your side do you always use

it? Help, My help is always ready and able to help you. To receive you must first believe, believe until there is true knowing.

BELOVED, your growth is limited by your time and attention given to Me. Pay attention to the fact of My constant presence. I rise with you in the morning, yes I've watched over you all night! Do you give Me that much time?

FREE GIFT

THERE IS A GIFT GIVEN TO MAN
ONE HE SELDOM USES,
A GIFT OF GREAT DESIRE
SO FREQUENTLY MAN ABUSES.

A GIFT SO SUBTLE IT'S IGNORED
A PRESENT VERY EXPENSIVE,
WRAPPED IN LOVE FROM UP ABOVE
THE WORLD VIEWS IT REPREHENSIVE.

NOW MY CHILD LOOK AT THIS GIFT
AND SEE WHAT ALL IT HOLDS,
BECAUSE ETERNAL LIFE IS WRAPPED
IN LOVE, LOVE THAT ISN'T SOLD!

MAN IS GIVEN ETERNAL LIFE
AND CHOICE OF WHERE TO EXIST,
TO BE WITH GOD IN HEAVEN
OR IN HELL AND HEAVEN MISSED!

BELOVED, why isn't My offer of life eternal so wonderful to man that he would do anything to receive it? Isn't this just the most wonderful news anyone on earth [seeing how short life is] could ever receive? Why don't you try harder to sell it?

BELOVED, have you ever set down with Me and just asked what can I do just for you Jesus?

BELOVED, thank you for reading all these little notes and thoughts each day. I truly hope you are helped be them, there must be and end you know! What will be your end?

THE END

WHAT TRULY IS THE END OF MAN?
CAN ANYONE REALLY KNOW?
WHERE GOES EACH SOUL AND SPIRIT
WHEN FLESH COMES TO THE "GO"?

WE SEE THE FLESH WEAR OUT AND DIE,
WE SEE CASKETS COME AND GO,
BUT WHAT IS THE END OF MAN?
WHEN FILLING GRAVES WITH DIRT WE THROW?

MAN SO VIBRANT FILLED WITH LIFE,
THEN FLESH JUST WITHERS AWAY.
WHERE GOES THAT LIFE SO HAPPY?
WHERE WILL EACH PERSON STAY?

THERE IS AN END TO ALL WE KNOW,
AND END THAT ALL MUST FACE.
DO YOU HAVE PEACE ABOUT THE END?
DO YOU REALLY KNOW THAT PLACE?

After enjoying this book, other books written by
Scott E. Beemer include:

SonRise Glories
Morning Glories
Eternal Glories
Lovable Glories
Beloved Glories
End Time Glories
(Soon to be released)

You can order these through your favorite bookstore or by con-
tacting Black Forest Press at (888) 808-5440 or
fax your order to (619) 482-8704. You may also order from
the shopping cart on our Web site at www.blackforestpress.com,
or send your orders to
Black Forest Press Marketing and Sales Department
914 Nolan Way
Chula Vista, CA 91910

To Contact Scott Beemer
Write To God's Open Forum
Box No. 80786
San Diego, CA 92138-0786
www.itsbeensold.com
You can also order Scott's books at this Web site.

Printed in the United States
1043500002B

9 781582 751146